Contents

Cover and title page: Two young kittens whose eyes have not yet achieved their permanent color.

This book is based upon Marjorie Farnham Schrody's *Cats*. It has been edited and thoroughly revised with additional material in the form of new captions and completely new color photography.

ISBN 0-87666-817-1

Distributed in the U.S. by T.F.H. Publications, Inc., 211 West Sylvania Avenue, PO Box 427, Neptune, NJ 07753; in England by T.F.H. (Gt. Britain) Ltd., 13 Nutley Lane, Reigate, Surrey; in Canada to the pet trade by Rolf C. Hagen Ltd., 3225 Sartelon Street, Montreal 382, Quebec; in Canada to the book trade by H & L Pet Supplies, Inc., 27 Kingston Crescent, Kitchener, Ontario N28 2T6; in Southeast Asia by Y.W. Ong, 9 Lorong 36 Geylang, Singapore 14; in Australia and the South Pacific by Pet Imports Pty. Ltd., P.O. Box 149, Brookvale 2100, N.S.W. Australia; in South Africa by Valid Agencies, P.O. Box 51901, Randburg 2125 South Africa. Published by T.F.H. Publications, Inc., Ltd., the British Crown Colony of Hong Kong.

The T.F.H. Book of KITTENS

t.f.h.

Marjorie F. Schrody

J. R. Spies's magnificent photo of a yawning black feline on the facing page contrasts nicely with the Persian longhair shown above.

The common "alley cat" kittens shown below make great pets too—especially if you acquire them as kittens.

Why You Should Have Cats in Your Home

Why should you have a cat—or two? There are many good reasons for owning cats, but the most important reason is that cats are likable and very adaptable. They are as comfortable in a furnished room as in a fifteen-room mansion—only you can put more of them into a mansion!

Cats are clean, the cleanest of all domesticated animals, and they do not have any odor. They are resourceful and more or less accept what comes in life. They adjust readily and seem to match their waking hours with yours. Their antics can amuse you, but if you just want to sit and relax, that suits them to a "T" too.

Cats like men, women, children, other cats, dogs, almost anything. They like all sorts of food. They like comfort, but they find it almost anywhere. Most cats travel well. They have a minimum of trouble giving birth. They are independent enough to live their own lives, yet affectionate enough to want your company.

Cats can be had free or for fabulous prices, and they come in all colors, sizes and temperaments. Let me note here that a "plain ol' cat" is just as nice and just as friendly and affectionate as a pure-bred.

A cat is one of the least expensive animals to keep as a pet. Generally the initial investment is low—most of the equipment you need such as dishes and a pan you probably already have in the house or can purchase at reasonable prices at your local pet shop.

Cats are graceful and lovely to watch in action. With their natural agility, developed as they pass through kittenhood, they manage to live in a home without breaking your favorite knickknacks.

There are many ridiculous and false superstitions about cats. Cats do not "suck baby's breath away" or anything of the kind. If a cat is near a baby's face, the cat is probably being affectionate. Cats don't bother with things they don't like; they just enjoy being close to "their" people.

Cats do *not* have nine lives. They do have an almost miraculous faculty for getting themselves out of predicaments, because of their natural resourcefulness and their lithe bodies. Their whiskers act as feelers and distance gauges. Their supple backbones bend and have flexible cartilage, thus they are more easily compressed and expanded than human spines. Their stomachs have an automatic "reverse gear" that enables them to regurgitate unsuitable "foods."

Cats do not eat rats. They will eat mice if they have to, but only hungry cats will eat them; and hungry cats can't catch many, as a cat doesn't hunt very well on an empty stomach. Cats, even the best mousers, must have a balanced diet—milk and mice are not adequate. Do not get a cat with the idea that since your house is mouse-infested, the cat will have a full belly all the time. A cat will catch more mice faster if it is a well-fed cat. A cat with a mousing heritage obviously makes a better mouser than a cat descended from a long line of non-mousers, but it is largely instinctive for any cat to catch mice.

Cats are smart, and not unfaithful. They do not, and will not, stay with cruel people just for a meal. They must be loved and appreciated to be at their best. They will let you know when danger is present and comfort you when you feel downcast. Make a mistake and they'll tell you about it—but they are quick to forgive.

Cats are smart. They are not unfaithful, but if children abuse them, the cats will stay away from the children and might even scratch them! Photo by Sally Anne Thompson. Below: A beautiful cream tabby Persian. Such long-haired cats may cost more than the more common short-haired cats, but they all make great pets. Photo by Fritz Prenzel.

There are a number of different cat species which are kept as pets. This young lady has a pet ocelot. It is almost impossible to obtain ocelots as pets, since they have been protected from capture in their native habitat and they are not being bred. But you can settle for a pair of "wild" kittens which may have been abandoned by their mother (below). Ask your local pet shop for the best source of kittens.

If you live in the country, a local farmer might be more than happy to get rid of some of his barn cats, but these usually are difficult to tame and train, since they have almost been living wild as barn animals and are usually shy. Barn cats, as a rule, are generally good mousers. Photo by Reinhard.

Where and How to Get a Cat

Once you are sure you want a cat and can give it a good home, you can decide whether you want to take a free cat or want to buy one, whether you want a particular breed or will take or buy any breed, whether you want a pure-bred pedigreed cat or will take or buy one without a heritage.

If you set your heart on a particular breed or a pedigreed cat, you will undoubtedly have to wait longer and do more searching to get what you want than if you accept a cat from an animal shelter or a friend or buy one from the first pet shop you enter.

No matter where you get your cat, have the animal's health checked by a veterinarian.

FREE CATS

Animal shelters usually have cats of all descriptions looking for homes. You won't get a pedigree, but you may be lucky enough to get a pure-bred cat. (Incidentally, a pedigree itself isn't soft and cuddly.) In fact, some shelters have a special service so that you can leave a general description of the cat you want, and you will be notified when one comes in. The shelter may or may not require a small monetary donation for each animal you take home as a pet.

Some of your friends may have cats, and if you get a cat from a friend you will know if the cat has been well taken care of, if its surroundings are clean and neat, and so forth. Friends' cats are usually free cats.

If you live in a rural area, a local farmer may have an excess number of cats for his barns. Chances are good that he'll give his permission for a kitten or two to leave the old homestead. These cats may not be as well fed as house cats and they may have worms (worms are relatively easy to cure), but they will be basically hardy cats and able to endure most conditions. Barn cats, as a rule, are good mousers.

You may also acquire a stray cat. A stray is a cat without a home, a cat that has been abandoned. A stray may follow you home, or you may simply find one in your yard or on your doorstep one day. You should be careful not to take someone else's cat, thinking it's a stray. A plump sleek cat, even though it may be out roaming, is not a stray—it's almost sure to belong to someone. Cats with collars are, of course, not strays.

House cats usually play with catnip mice more often than with real mice. Pouncing on small moving objects is a natural instinct with cats. Photo by Sally Anne Thompson.

11

Be particularly wary of bringing in a stray if you already have kittens or cats in your home. Your own cats should be vaccinated against feline enteritis first. The stray should be kept secluded until it has been inoculated and the veterinarian has ascertained its health. It is important to bring a stray immediately to the veterinarian to minimize infections from any possible contagious diseases.

BUYING FROM A PET SHOP

If there is a pet shop in your vicinity, your search for a cat may be ended. Go in and look around. Proper cleanliness, heating and feeding are marks of a good pet shop. Talk to the manager. If the store does not have the type of cat you want or if the store does not have any cats, ask the manager if he can get you the kind you are looking for.

While you're at the pet shop, look around at the displays and shelves of the store. Here you'll be able to get the things you'll need to help you take good care of your cat.

BUYING FROM A BREEDER

The best way to buy a pure-bred cat is directly from a breeder, preferably one in your vicinity (to eliminate shipping). You can get names and addresses from a pet shop, by reading the classified ads in a newspaper or specialty magazine or by going to a cat show and taking down the names of breeders. If you want to buy a cat seen at a show, wait about three weeks so that if the cat has caught any indisposition while being exhibited, it will have recovered.

Cats from a breeder will be pedigreed, and at the time of purchase you should receive a document stating the pedigree. Sometimes you will not be able to get the pedigree document for a male cat until you produce a certificate from a veterinarian saying that you have had the animal neutered.

A good cat will not be too **cheap**, so **beware of bargains**. On the other hand, the cat with the highest price tag isn't always the best either; because of his fancy breeding he may be too high-strung for a family cat. Females are usually cheaper than males, and the runt of the litter will be the cheapest of all. If you and a kitten hit it off, get the kitten. You'll both be happy.

MORE THAN ONE KITTEN?

If you are planning to get a cat, you might do what many people do: get two of them. They then have each other for company. Of course, the cat has *you*, but would you like it if you never saw another human? If possible (and it usually is), get littermates. They are already fast friends and have no period of adjustment to go through. They are no extra work and are more than twice the fun.

Lots of cats are left to roam for themselves. Many unthinking people leave their cats when they move from a fairly large house to a small apartment where cats may not be welcome. For some reason, cats love to hide under cars. The cat you find under your car might well be a stray or a neighbor's cat out for the evening. It is best not to adopt strays.

J. R. Spies is a noted cat photographer. Here he has captured his cat taking a long stretch after a short nap! Cats have some very dramatic poses if you are able to capture them on film.

A quartet of Siamese cats, showing different color varieties.

Top facing page: A
Himalayan. Photo by Sally
Anne Thompson. Bottom,
facing page: An orange-
eyed white Persian.

What Kind of Cat?

There are many varieties of cats, but only the more prominent breeds will be discussed here.

Of all cats, there are two major divisions: longhairs and shorthairs.

LONGHAIRS

Of the accepted and registerable longhairs in the United States today, the Persian and Himalayan are probably the most popular. The Turkish Angora, another longhair, is not yet commonly available. Longhairs require more grooming than shorthairs, but they are just as affectionate as pets.

Persian—The Persian is big, with long, thick hair. Despite its massiveness, it is a quiet cat, although a playful kitten. The eyes of a good Persian always contrast with its body color, and there are many body colors.

Himalayan—The Himalayan looks like a Persian cat with Siamese markings. In fact, the Himalayan was the result of crossbreeding Persian and Siamese cats. Himalayans have blue eyes and have color names (like Siamese cats, described below) which reflect the color of their feet, tail, ears and mask.

SHORTHAIRS

The most prominent of the shorthairs are the Siamese, American Shorthair, Manx, Abyssinian and Burmese.

Siamese—A lithe, svelte smart-as-a-whip devil, the Siamese is guaranteed to be your constant friend and counselor. Siamese are given a color name in accord with the color of their "points"—feet, tail, ears and mask. Siamese colors recognized by most shows and cat clubs are: Seal, Chocolate, Blue and Lilac.

Siamese kittens are born pure white; they gradually change color and gain points as they grow older. They develop full coloring earlier than one year of age; then their body color darkens with age until at about five years it changes no more. The coat remains sleek and not the least bit fluffy after the cat leaves the kitten stage.

Siamese are noted for their bright blue, slightly slanted eyes. The body of the Siamese is angular, with a slightly elevated rump set on long, slender hind legs. The feet are small and dainty, the Seal Points having dark pads. The head is wedge-like in shape.

The Siamese are talkative cats, more so than any other breed. Their gutteral squawks follow you from attic to basement as they continually air their views on life, which some people find annoying. Siamese are noted too for their personality quirks. No two are alike, and no one cat is typical of the breed.

American Shorthair—Commonly known as Domestic Shorthair, this now-recognized breed has risen to its own in the United States. The cat's head is large, with wide, round eyes. The fur is dense and soft. Color combinations as well as solid colors are accepted in the registry, and any and all colors are available. Tabby and Tortoiseshell (white, black and red) are the most common combinations. The breed is hardy and fastidious, and it typifies the word "cat" for many Americans.

Manx—Originally from the Isle of Man, these tailless cats are a most unusual breed. Their hind legs are long and attenuated, and their rumps large and meaty. A true Manx has a depression where its tail should be. At some shows now we find Manx cats with flat rumps or just the trace of a first joint. The Manx usually comes in Gray Tabby, although almost all colors can be accounted for. They make gay companions and are most amusing.

Abyssinian—Descended from Egyptian sacred cats, this breed is very unusual and quite expensive. Their beautiful voices are used infrequently, and so they are among the quietest of cats. Abyssinians are basically ruddy brown or red, each ticked with darker shades, making them lovely to look at. They are quite playful and amuse themselves for hours on end.

Burmese—The Burmese are very similar to the Siamese in body shape and in character, but Burmese are solid brown, with hazel or golden eyes. They are most affectionate and love playing and people. They are harder to find than the Siamese, but quite a few breeders in this country offer them for sale.

The common alley cat has been recognized as a breed all its own. It is called the "American Shorthair" in America, but it is often called a "Foreign Shorthair" in Britain. The black specimen above has yellow eyes. The foreign white shown below is climbing up a tree. Photo by Sally Anne Thompson. The cat on the facing page is a longhaired mixed breed.

MALE VS. FEMALE

Distinguishing males from females seems to present a problem to the amateur as the male kitten's testicles are not readily noticed. However, if you turn up the kitten's tail and examine its underside (the seller won't mind), you can reassure yourself as to the gender. The male will have a "colon" (:) while the female will have an "exclamation point" upside down (¡). This is the easiest way to differentiate the sexes, and it works quite well.

Whether to get a male or a female is another matter. As kittens, the differences are negligible. Both are cute, playful

THE WORLD'S LARGEST SELECTION OF PET, ANIMAL, AND MUSIC BOOKS.

T.F.H. Publications publishes more than 900 books covering many hobby aspects (dogs, cats, birds, fish, small animals, music, etc.). Whether you are a beginner or an advanced hobbyist you will find exactly what you're looking for among our complete listing of books. For a free catalog fill out the form on the other side of this page and mail it today.

. . . ANIMALS . . .

. . . BIRDS . . .

. . . CATS . . .

. . . DOGS . . .

. . . FISH . . .

. . . MUSIC . . .

Above: A magnificent Burmese cat whose name is Mizpah's Trotsky of G(len)n. It is owned by Glenn Roggerson and Len White. Len White took the photograph. To the left is an American Shorthair whose colors are tortoiseshell and white. All tortoiseshell cats are females, since that color is sex-linked and sex-limited to the female gene combination.

The illustration to the right shows the belly of a cat that has been neutered. The practice of tattooing a neutered animal has been proposed by the American Veterinary Medical Association. Photo courtesy of *Journal of the American Veterinary Medical Association*.

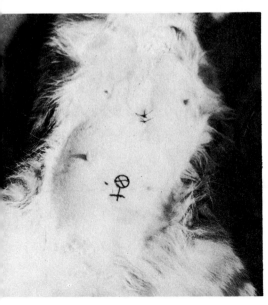

and adorable, but the males tend to be a little more aggressive. It is when they grow up that you may wish you'd picked either "Susie's cute little brother" or "Tom's cute little sister."

Although many people feel that either sex will make a good house cat, I feel that a female makes a better house cat than a male. She will stay in the house and never need to go out, and she will be friendlier, cozier, more affectionate and quieter than a male (except when she is in heat). When she comes into heat, at about nine months of age, she'll meow, yowl, dash from door to window and back again, and crouch with her tail up. This active stage lasts about a week and occurs from one to eight times a year.

If you do not plan to breed your female cat, she should be spayed. This complex operation is not dangerous anymore, due to modern aseptic surgical techniques. The cat is generally kept hospitalized until ready to go home. After a female is spayed, she will never come into heat, and she will be much, much easier to live with.

A female will be very clean and not get into fights—only cause them! If she goes out of the house, she will have kittens regularly unless you have her spayed. Spaying makes her remain a kitten longer and does not make her fat and lazy—eating too much and not exercising enough do that. Females are more gentle generally and not as easily distracted as males.

Toms grow bigger and stronger than their sisters, but they are no hardier. A male will never present you with a batch of kittens, but he may be used for stud after one year. A male may not cuddle up as a female does on long evenings. He'd rather be out on the town! A male *has* to go out. If he goes out, he will not mess up the house, but he may stay out for long hours or days at a stretch.

If your male can't go out, he should be neutered (castrated) when he comes of age, which is at about six months. When his testicles descend fully, have him neutered by your veterinarian. This is a simple and inexpensive operation. Your cat will stay at home thereafter and be a companion instead of wanderer.

While any cat at all can be housebroken, the unaltered male will "spray" (from his anal glands) a musky-smelling liquid into every nook and cranny of your house. The odor is permanent and meant to attract females. An unaltered male will also forget his toilet training at times and urinate against the walls, in corners or any place that takes his fancy.

With a neutered cat, you'll never be bothered by spraying and yowling. Since a neutered male presents no problems at all, you may prefer to buy a male kitten if you are not interested in breeding but merely want to be a cat owner and lover.

PEDIGREES AND REGISTRATIONS

There are several organizations that maintain lists of registered cats, and the cat may be registered with one or all of these associations.

Once a cat is registered, its pedigree may be kept in the organization's books. The pedigree is the chart of a cat including its name and breed with as much of its ancestry as the owner knows. The association sends a form for registration to each cat owner who applies. The information on the registration form will include age, sex, date of birth, coloring, description of all sorts, its dam and sire (mother and father), owner, breeder and ancestry. If the ancestry is unknown, you can simply state "Unknown" in the proper place.

Each of these associations also maintains a foundation record. This is for cats who have a known ancestry for three or four generations. The ancestors must also have been included in the stud book. The offspring of cats who have been registered in the stud book for three or four generations are automatically included in the foundation record.

Ron Reagan's photo of a Russian Blue, Ch. Nordic Ingrid

Fritz Prenzel's photo of two Abyssinians: a ruddy and a red.

Feeding

THE FIRST YEAR

If you have a mother cat, she'll take care of the whole feeding process. She'll watch what the kittens eat, how much and when. She'll teach them to lap up milk, teach them which foods are good and teach them not to touch spoiled food. Until the kittens are about two months old, the mother will gradually wean them with bits of her own food.

Little kittens up to four weeks of age should, if their mother is running out of milk, be given small supplementary feedings of a warmed milk mixture as often as they need it. There are specially prepared milk-substitute products for feeding newborn kittens, and the directions on the package will tell you how much to feed and when to do the feeding.

If your kittens were old enough to leave their mother when you got them, then you shouldn't have much of a problem. The only questions will be how many times a day and how much you need to feed them. If the mother cat is not around, keep feeding the kittens milk only until their first teeth appear. Then about four times a day give them each a teaspoonful of canned cat food, scraped meat or baby food, with two teaspoonsful of egg-and-milk mixture—a total of about four ounces a day.

As your kittens get older, give each a couple of table-spoonsful of solid food at a feeding, about four feedings a day. If this schedule is impossible to maintain, give them a little more food and feed them no less than three times a day. A decent diet consists of milk and egg mixed together for breakfast; baby food, beef or commercially prepared cat food for lunch; and milk and egg plus commercial cat food for supper—up to about six ounces a day. When the kittens are over six months old, feed them three times a day, and after about eight months of age, twice a day would be fine. The minimum amount of food a cat should be offered is between five and eight ounces a day, depending on the size of your cat.

WATER

Clean, fresh water should always be available for your pet, and the water bowl should be washed each day. The water should be provided at *all* times, not only at feeding times.

VITAMIN AND MINERAL SUPPLEMENTS

Supplements of vitamins and minerals should be added to a kitten's diet at an early age. By providing a balanced diet and by using such supplements at the dosage recommended on the packaging, you will be sure that your kitten is getting all of its nutritional requirements.

COMMERCIAL FOODS

There are various commercial foods formulated especially for kittens, so when you begin to add commercial cat food to your kitten's diet, make sure the food you purchase is designed for kittens. Once your kitten matures, commercial cat foods will probably be its main source of nutrition. Since cat food is available in several forms (dry, moist or canned) you'll be able to supply your pet with a variety of textures at the same time you provide a variety of flavors. It is important to vary your pet's diet so that you will be sure that all of its nutritional needs are met and too it does not become "addicted" to only one type, flavor or brand of cat food.

EGGS AND MILK

Eggs and milk can be a part of a growing kitten's diet, but they should never be your pet's only food.

Eggs contain important vitamins and minerals, and many cats enjoy eggs, either raw or cooked. Many people believe that a cat should be fed one raw egg a week for nutritional purposes and also to give its coat a glossy sheen. Only the yolk of the egg should be fed, and it can be fed "as is" or mixed with milk. The white of a raw egg should be avoided as it may be harmful to the cat.

Milk can fulfill some of the nutritional needs of your pet, but milk is not an essential element of an adult cat's diet. Milk, evaporated or whole, mixed with water or "straight", can be fed to your kitten or cat, but your pet may have trouble digesting it and the result may be indigestion or diarrhea. You can try feeding your cat about two teaspoonsful of milk a day and see how your pet reacts to it. If the milk upsets its digestive system, try reducing the amount of milk or eliminate it from the diet entirely.

TABLE SCRAPS

In general, most cats enjoy eating some table scraps, or human food, but you should be judicious about which scraps you feed. Whichever human foods you feed your pet, don't give them in excessive amounts or to the exclusion of any other foods.

Many cats like to nibble on cheese, bread, cake or even melon. Fish is a favorite food, but only cooked fish should be fed (and, of course, the bones should be removed).

Above: Most cats love milk even though it is not essential for their diet once they have matured. This feeding dish has an advantage in the kitchen, for the "drip pan" catches the drops that may fall from your pet's mouth after it drinks. On the facing page is a gorgeous photo of two kittens terrorizing two goldfish! Kittens have a natural tendency to claw anything that is small and moves fast. They are, therefore, dangerous to goldfish.

The best food for a kitten is usually supplied by its mother, but as the young family members mature (especially those in a large family), a bit of help from the owner is warranted. In the photo below, a Burmese is very apprehensive about eating. Note the crouched position with its tail tucked under its body.

Vegetables, either cooked or raw, are usually enjoyed by cats, and some will relish tomatoes. A small amount of fat is good for a cat, so a little animal fat or butter may be beneficial.

Spicy foods are not for cats. Most of my own cats have a passion for ravioli. The minute they smell it, they come leaping up onto the table and steal it from under my very nose! I usually let them have a drop or two of the sauce and then shoo them away. I don't let them lick the plates (even when they tell me how cruel and heartless I am), because there is too much sauce there. It is hard to resist plaintive "meows" and accusing stares, but it is even harder to nurse a sick cat!

DISHES AND EATING HABITS

Your cats should have their own set of dishes and these should be thoroughly washed and rinsed well after each meal. Don't leave food sitting in them; remove the dishes about twenty minutes after the cats have stopped eating. This gives them time to come back, if they decide they want more. If the food is left exposed for a longer period, it will turn rancid and develop an unpleasant odor. All you should leave down for your pets is fresh water and an occasional cat biscuit as a treat.

Try to feed your cats at approximately the same hour every day. Cats are creatures of habit and get hungry at regular intervals. They'll be healthier with regular feedings.

Some cats are problem eaters—they don't like one thing, something else gives them a rash, and so on and so forth. With this kind of eater, if it isn't a matter of tastes, it is advisable to take the cat to a competent veterinarian, who will perhaps give the cat tests and give you a few feeding suggestions. If it is a matter of likes and dislikes, the easy way out is, of course, to follow the line of least resistance and feed the cat what it likes (provided the food isn't harmful). Otherwise, offer the regular food at the regular time. If your cat just sniffs at the food and strolls off, it might not be hungry. Pick up the food and reserve it for the next meal. If your cat won't eat but scratches at the floor, trying to cover up the food, it wants something better or the food might be tainted.

If your cat won't eat for three days, and the food is neither spoiled nor rancid, and you know it hasn't been getting any other food, take the cat to your veterinarian, as it may be coming down with something more serious than a cold.

Most cats like baby food. It is especially good for old cats whose teeth are not so strong and for very young kittens. Expensive, but nourishing, it can be mixed with water or fed straight from the jar.

Three black kittens have been weaned early and have been introduced to commercial food. If you want to check the entire variety of commercially prepared cat foods, make sure you visit a pet shop—pet shops have specially prepared cat foods that aren't available in supermarkets.

When purchasing cat foods, check the labels; you want a food that is rich in protein (meat or fish), not high in carbohydrates (wheat and corn products).

If your pet watches you eating steak when all the cat has is a dish of cat food, don't be surprised if it thinks you are a cruel monster. If it can't cajole you out of a morsel or two, and can't steal any, your cat will probably give you a killing look and then sit and sulk. My conscience won't let me eat steak without sharing. One look at my cats—even though I know the swaying from "starvation," half-closed eyes, weak little cries and all the rest, are an act—and I cut off a little bit of steak for them. This is enough. They don't (usually!) want to rob me; they just want a taste. Then they go back to their own food and I can eat in peace. Sometimes it's worth it.

CARE

BRINGING YOUR KITTEN HOME

After eight weeks, a kitten of any breed but Siamese may be taken from its mother into a new home. (Siamese remain kittens for a long time. Even though their eyes open the earliest of any breeds, they are slower to develop physiologically. Siamese are excellent mothers and usually have an abundant supply of milk. A Siamese can be removed from its mother when three months old.)

When you first get the kitten home, put it down and let it alone. Put a small bowl of water down, show the newcomer where its litter pan is, and don't give it anything to eat.

The kitten probably won't have a bowel movement for twelve hours or so, or it may be rushing to the pan every few minutes. This latter is caused by nervousness and the transition, and is considered a normal condition. It may urinate—probably frequently. This will accustom it to its new pan. If it is very frightened and makes a mess on the floor, *do not* punish it. The kitten will be too scared to understand, and you will only make matters worse. Move the kitten to its sleeping box and calmly clean up the mess. There is no sense in putting the kitten in its pan now, because the kitten no longer needs it. Do that the next time!

When nighttime comes, your little kitten will probably cry. If it is a Siamese, you won't get any sleep. If it is of another breed, you may be able to sleep if you are hardhearted. For all concerned, it is a good idea to move the kitten's box near your bed. (You can put the kitten in bed with you, but once a cat sleeps on a bed, it is the start of a lifelong habit. The cat will want to curl up with you ever after.) If you put the kitten's bed by your bed, you can reach a hand down and comfort the kitten, or you can wrap a hot water bottle in a towel and lay it in the box, *flat under the kitten.* If you stand it up, it may fall down and suffocate the kitten. A ticking clock has been said to help kittens to adjust, as it simulates the mother cat's heartbeat and is a constant reassuring noise.

Bear in mind that no cat, especially a kitten, will behave in its new home as it did when you picked it out. At times, the first few days are very discouraging. Koki, one of our Siamese queens, was as sweet as pie while with her mother, but the minute she set paw inside our door she was vicious. After a week of love and affection we could approach her without being forced to wear leather gloves. Now she is one of our most affectionate cats and loves one and all.

If you bring a kitten home, be sure to be prepared for it. Your pet shop will have beds, flea collars and a dozen other little items you'll need to make your new kitten that much more comfortable.
Don't forget feeding dishes. Photo by Sally Anne Thompson.
The tabby on the facing page prefers to have its food hidden in the bushes. Cats are often very private about eating and will take their food away to a private place to eat it.

Your newly located kitten is frightened and lonesome. It will need a bit of time to learn where its pan, food and bed are and to familiarize itself with the surroundings. Give it a day or two (generally) and the kitten will act as though it owns the place.

Limit the kitten's territory to one or two rooms, or some other small area, when you first bring it home. This will keep it from getting "lost" and help its peace of mind (and yours). After it is familiar with you, then let it explore the house. Go with it the first time, just in case it gets into something it can't get out of. The kitten won't be happy until it has gone over every nook and cranny with a fine tooth comb! Then after it is acclimated, the kitten will be happier.

If the kitten is going to be an indoor-outdoor cat, don't let it out until it is sure of itself in the house. When you do let it out, go with it the first two or three times—until it gains its sense of direction and knows where the door is.

The second morning your kitten is with you it should be hungry. It will eat, explore and get into mischief. Once it has been fed by you, however humble the fare, the kitten will be your buddy.

Give the kitten a small quantity of milk, either "straight" or mixed with water, as its first feeding in its new territory. Warm the milk to at least room temperature, but be careful not to make it too hot; test it on your wrist, as you would for an infant. After the initial feeding, you can start right in feeding the food suggested in the previous chapter.

THE KITTEN'S BED

Each kitten and cat should have its own bed—a place where it can be alone to think and sleep or do whatever cats do in their off moments. There are special cat baskets available at pet shops which work very well. These cat baskets or boxes come in many different designs and sizes, and you'll be able to find one that is perfect for your cat. You can make your own cat bed by taking a cardboard carton, with one side cut down for accessibility, and pad it with an old, clean towel or a doll- or baby-blanket, but this homemade box will probably not hold up for very long and, frankly, it won't look as nice as any of those available at your pet shop. The padding inside the basket, or bed, can be removed for washing; just be sure to put in a substitute while you are doing the washing.

When your kitten or cat is in its basket, it wants privacy. When it wants company, it will come and seek you out.

HOT AND COLD

Cats like it warm, and cats can stand heat better than most animals. If you have radiators, a piece of plywood

Each kitten should have a bed of its own. Your pet shop will have a special basket-type bed as shown above. Photo by Sally Anne Thompson.

If you own more than one cat you won't need separate dishes for each one even though you might need separate beds for each. This mother cat cleans her kitten while they eat. The mother below is bringing one of her kits back to safety after it started to wander.

A beautiful pair. The silver Persian contrasts nicely with the sealpoint Himalayan.
The long coats of these two breeds protect them from the cold, but they tend to
shed if kept in a warm house during the summer.

There are many ways to lift a kitten or fully grown cat. Certainly grabbing it by the tail is NOT one way, nor is getting a handful of the skin on the back of the neck. Gently lift your cat. Use two hands. One hand goes under the cat's chest and stomach while the other hand supports the feet and hind quarters as these two photographs show so clearly. Teach your children how to properly lift their cats. Sally Anne Thompson photos.

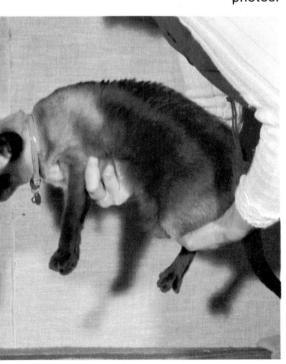

over the top of one will give them a warm place to sit. Your cats may curl up on the register, in front of a space heater or in front of a roaring fire. Cats take changes in temperature well, too—from inside to outside and back again. Generally your cats will catch a cold only from a draft or a drastic temperature change—that is, if they are indoor cats and get out on an extremely cold day. Most of the time, however, cats can run in the snow and then come and curl up by the hottest place in the house with no ill effects.

WET AND DRY

Most cats prefer to be dry and appear to have a definite aversion to getting wet. There are, of course, exceptions. Pandora loves to curl up in the bathroom sink with the water running, and Coquette will jump into the bathtub whenever she hears splashing. However, neither of them venture outdoors in the slightest drizzle! If your cats or kittens have been outside in the rain and come back soaking wet, it is best to towel them dry and let them finish off the job by licking themselves. The toweling will make the job easier for them and will start their blood circulating faster to help prevent a chill. They should be kept out of drafts, but they will probably see to this themselves.

LIFTING

The correct way to lift up any cat is with two hands. Put one hand under the cat's chest and stomach, and use the other hand to support its feet. *Never* try to pick up a cat by the scruff of its neck and never by the stomach (or by any other single part of the body) alone.

HOUSEBREAKING

Cats are the easiest of domestic animals to housebreak. Generally you won't even have to go through this phase. If a kitten has been with its mother for any length of time, she has taken care of it for you.

Most cats and kittens are trained to an indoor pan. Litter pans are available in several sizes and styles (some look like miniature houses) and many different colors. There are even inexpensive disposable ones on the market. Get one with sides low enough for the kitten to jump over and see above. The pan should be filled with one of the many different litters available at the pet store. Some litter products are now chemically treated to prevent odors. Materials such as sawdust or sand are not good to use in the pan because the kitten will get particles in its paws, eyes and fur (and consequently into its stomach), to say nothing of tracking it all over the house.

The contents of the pan should either be sifted or changed every day, as kittens and cats don't care to use a dirty pan any more than you like to have one around. If the pan gets too dirty, your pet may use the floor or the rug as a not-too-subtle hint for you to clean up.

If your kitten is not trained to use a pan when you first get it, show your new pet where the pan is and then take the kitten's paws in your hand and make digging motions with them until you have dug a little hole. Then sit the kitten on it. The kitten may not have to use the pan at that moment, but at least your pet will get the right idea. Don't change the location of the pan without making sure your kitten knows where it is. This safeguards against accidents.

Every week or so scrub the pan with a brush and hot, soapy water. This prevents germs and bacteria from developing and helps to keep the pan clean and sweet-smelling for you and your kitten. A little baking soda in the bottom of the pan, underneath the litter material, will also help to check odors. Don't use a strong disinfectant to clean the pan, because the disinfectant may be toxic to cats, and the smell might actually repel the cat from the pan.

If you decide eventually to let your kitten or cat go outdoors to perform its daily duties, go out with your pet the first few times. Show the kitten a patch of dirt and dig its claws in the dirt, so it'll realize the purpose of the trip.

A couple I know had a Manx named Tau who would go outside and then scratch on the screen to come in again. When let in, he would run to his pan, use it and then ask to go out again. They kept moving the pan nearer and nearer to the door and eventually moved it outside. They finally dispensed with it altogether and let Tau use the great outdoors, which never needs emptying.

A cat will never dirty its sleeping box or any other place that is its "domain." Cats are naturally clean animals.

GROOMING

Your kitten or cat should be brushed every day if it is a shorthair, twice a day if it is a longhair and more frequently in the fall and spring when the coat is changing and shedding a lot. Brushing helps you by leaving less hair for the cat to shed on the furniture. It helps the cat because as it licks it swallows hair and this invites the danger of hair balls (discussed more fully later).

Most cats like to be brushed, although some don't want their stomachs or chests touched and, in protest, will dig into you with their hind feet. Start brushing your pet regularly from the time you get it as a kitten. Cats like routine and enjoy sitting on your lap and being stroked. Tomcats may not like to have their fur brushed upward. With longhairs, it is advisable to brush the fur both ways, as the soft under-coat sheds too, and by brushing in all directions you get more hair out. If your cat is shedding quite a lot, rub a

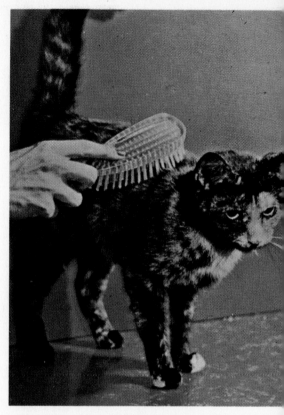

Your cat or kitten should be brushed as often as possible. Daily brushing is certainly a minimum if you want to keep the shed hairs from accumulating all over your home. Long-haired cats should be brushed twice a day. While grooming your cat be sure you use the proper brush. Your pet shop has special cat brushes. Below: Trim your cat's nails from time to time, too. Ask your pet shop for a special cat nail clipper.

Right: Your pet shop might have a two-sided brush which will have ample strength and penetrating power to remove tangles as well as dead hair. Photo by Sally Anne Thompson. Below: This cat is "spraying," thus the awkward position, but its disheveled coat indicates it needs better grooming.

damp cloth over the cat's coat to help remove the excess hairs.

At pet shops there are brushes designed especially for cats. These brushes remove a lot of hair and are the right size for getting under the chin, on top of the head and so on. Use a different brush for each cat, and clean the brushes frequently. Pull the hair out of the brush after each grooming session and every two weeks or so wash the brush in warm water.

Do not use brushes designed for dogs. These are too stiff and too large for a kitten or small cat.

BATHING

Cats keep themselves fairly clean; they "bathe" all the time. There are, however, cats like Regal Prince (a Siamese) who washes and washes and washes—but always the same paw! If he gets dirty, he lets one of his playmates clean up! Most cats, after you've spent time brushing them, will walk away in disgust and will give themselves a *good* "bath," with contempt in their eyes for human methods.

If a cat should get really dirty, from soot, mud or the like, it may be necessary to give it a bath. A cat should not be bathed too often, as this dries out the natural oils of the skin. Moreover, most cats don't care for the process.

When you bathe your cat, put a few inches of warm, clear water in your bathtub or kitchen sink. Put a dish towel or rubber mat in the bottom so the cat will have something other than your arms to dig its claws into. Use a soap formulated for use on cats, or a mild soap. Wet the cat all over, except its head, and be careful not to splash any water on its face or into its ears. Then, starting at the neck, pour on a small amount of the soap and make a lather; rub the lather down the backbone, from the neck to the base of the tail. Gradually work around to the sides and to the stomach, legs and paws. Do the tail last. If the cat's face is very dirty, lather the top of the head and then work down. *Be very careful not to get soap or water into the cat's eyes, nose, mouth or ears.*

Now comes the rinsing part. If you are fortunate enough to have a double sink, it simplifies matters, as you can lift the cat to the other sink into clear water. Otherwise, hold onto the cat well, lift it out of the sink (the cat may become frightened by the sound of the water draining out) and change the water. It should be necessary only to rinse the cat twice, but do make sure that all the soap comes out of the fur.

When your cat is clean again, towel it dry. You can rub the cat down (and calm it) by holding the cat on your lap as you dry it. Your cat may favor you with dirty looks galore or it may try to claw you a bit, but it'll soon forget the humiliation.

Cats are exceptionally clean animals, but if they get involved with paint, oil or any other material which might be dangerous to be licked off, then bathing is certainly indicated. Pet shops have special cat soaps, shampoos and even dry shampoos which are sprayed on and rubbed or brushed off. Photo by Sally Anne Thompson.

Your cat's hair should be glistening, shiny and healthy looking. These kittens have poor hair quality. Their diet should include vitamins and their coat must be brushed twice a day to keep it in good shape. Your cat's coat should be as shiny as a young girl's well-cared-for hair.

Cats must sharpen their claws, and they do this with a scratching post. Your pet shop will have many different kinds of scratching posts to show you.

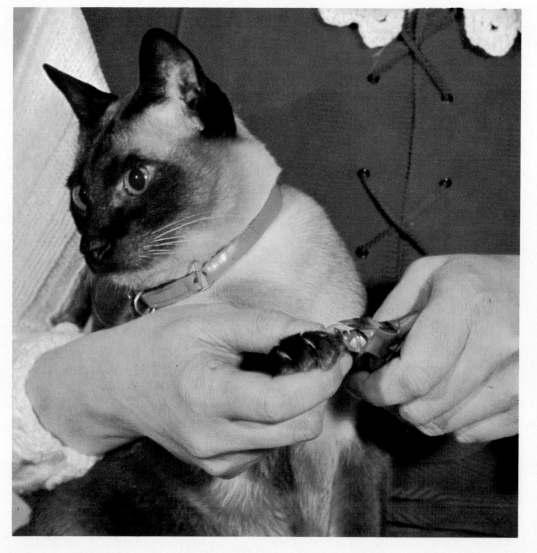

If your cat is allowed outdoors, it will probably wear its claws down in the natural process of walking and climbing and thus never require having its claws cut. But if the cat is restricted to your home, then it eventually will require that its claws be clipped. Special nail clippers are required. Your pet shop will usually have them. Photos on this page by Sally Anne Thompson.

Cats and kittens love toys, especially toys that move. Not all toys, however, are suitable; some can be dangerous. Pet shops carry a large assortment of safe toys.

PLAYTHINGS

All kittens and cats love toys. Old spools or balls of yarn will do nicely. Some kittens like soft cuddly toys; others like harder chewy ones. My cats like ping-pong balls because they roll in any direction at all. Pet stores handle toys of all kinds for cats and for a small cash investment you can keep your pet quite happy.

Kittens and cats like catnip, dried or as a fresh herb from a garden or in a flowerpot. A kitten or cat with a catnip mouse is amused (and amusing) for hours. Your pet will toss it, run after it, pounce on it, lick it and have loads of fun.

SCRATCHING POSTS

The scratching post is in a class separate from grooming or toys. The most simply designed scratching post is one which has an upright sturdy pole nailed to a square board that is big enough for the cat to sit on. Sometimes both sections are covered with carpeting. You can easily make one of these or buy one. Pet stores sell a variety of scratching posts; and they range from the simple pole and board affair to large, carpeted posts with platforms and tunnels. Many of these are sprinkled with oil of catnip to attract the cat to it.

A scratching post is a definite necessity for you and the cat, particularly if you keep your cat indoors most of the time. If the kitten or cat learns to sharpen its claws on the post, you won't have tattered rugs or torn upholstery, and it will keep the cat's nails trim. It is also good for the animal's muscle tone and will help keep your pet fit. Your cat will do its daily calisthenics there with no urging and be very amusing in the process.

Show your kitten where the post is and how to claw. Induce the kitten to claw the post either by putting its front feet on the post or by lifting the kitten up and letting it grab onto the post with all four feet. Your kitten will soon get the idea. Any time you see the kitten digging your rugs or furniture, bring the kitten to its post and help it use the post. In a very short time your pet will learn, and chances are it would rather use the post anyway, as it is firmer.

CLAW CARE

If your kitten or cat goes outdoors, its nails should never be cut at all, as they aid it in climbing and are its only defense against other animals. The climbing your pet does will keep its claws trim.

If you have an indoor cat, however—even one that regularly uses the scratching post you have provided—you will probably have to trim its claws, at least occasionally. Special cat claw clippers can be purchased from your local pet shop, but be sure that you know how to do the trimming properly. You have to clip off only a small bit of each claw on the front paws. If you cut off too much, you may accidentally cut the blood vessel which runs through each claw. If you are not sure how to go about trimming the claws, have your veterinarian show you how it's done.

COLLARS

Collaring cats is a much disputed subject. Collars on outdoor cats serve the purpose of telling people that this cat belongs to someone and is not a stray. If there is any identification on the collar, you stand a better chance of having your cat returned if the animal gets lost.

Almost any cat will accept a collar without much of a fuss. At first your cat may try to claw it off, but the cat soon will forget it is wearing one. Some cats (the showmen of the race) love a collar and parade around with it. If you tie a bow on the collar they strut all the higher. Most cats, however, are annoyed by a bow and will take measures to claw one off.

A collar on an outdoor cat however can be, and often is, very dangerous. Aside from the fact that collars on outdoor cats are a hindrance in fighting, many cats have been strangled while climbing trees—they slip and the collar catches over a branch. Some people advise using collars with elastic backs, as the cat can slip the collar over its head and jump free if it gets caught. These collars have a drawback, however; they are useless in training a cat to the leash—when you pull the leash the collar slips off.

A cat that is going to be leash-trained (discussed in detail later) has to wear a collar some of the time. The more the cat wears the collar, the sooner will it get used to it. If you're going to bother to leash-train your cat, it won't be running loose much anyway.

Check your kitten's collar every week and a half. A collar that is "just right" in size one day may suddenly be outgrown; kittens grow at an astounding rate.

The collar should not be so tight that it hinders the cat while eating or so loose that it accidentally catches the lower jaw while the cat is washing. If your cat should get its jaw caught, throw a jacket or towel over the animal to stop its thrashing about, and then remove the collar, cutting it if necessary. Calm the cat and (if possible) put the collar back on, one hole tighter than it was before.

Round leather collars or collars with soft felt backing are best, as a collar tends to wear away the hair on a cat's neck. If you get a flat collar, get a very narrow one. All cat collars should be light in weight.

Choke collars for cats are totally uncalled for. In theory they seem to be perfect: (1) the pressure is applied only when the cat pulls, and it lets up the minute the cat stops pulling; (2) when the cat is not on the leash, the collar hangs free and doesn't rub off the fine neck fur; (3) if the cat is caught on a tree, the collar will slip off over the cat's head; (4) since it works not by pulling but by choking, the cat is supposed to learn to walk on the leash better and faster; ad infinitum. This, however, is sadly not the case. A cat is a stubborn, independent animal and will choke itself to death before it will be pulled anywhere it doesn't want to go. When an ordinary collar is pulled, it will drag the cat rather than choke it, thereby eliminating all chance of accident. Also, if a cat gets its leash wrapped around something, as cats are prone to do, there is no danger of a slow and agonizing death with an ordinary collar.

"Poppit bead" collars that snap apart are good for outdoor cats but not for cats on leashes.

Flea collars are practical and are comparatively safe. They, however, must be replaced frequently. They are not meant to be used for anything except as a flea repellent.

There are harnesses sold which have been designed especially for cats. They eliminate all danger of choking and of sore necks. Many times a cat that won't walk on a leash when collared will respond with no trouble to a harness. Harnesses come in various sizes, but they are best used on adult cats. Even the smallest harness is probably too large for a kitten.

You can have lots of fun training your cat to a collar and leash right in your own home. Cats and kittens must have fresh air, and the only safe way to give your kittens some freedom is to walk them, especially if you live in an apartment or in a city where traffic poses a danger to a wandering kitten. Photo by Sally Anne Thompson.

A sealpoint Siamese proudly shows off its collar. Pet shops offer a wide variety of collars—including flea collars. Flea collars are necessary if your cat is allowed outdoors, where it is very likely to meet the neighborhood flea-ridden alley cat.

TRAINING

Training your kitten requires the patience of Job plus a lot of time. Your kitten will understand you, but being a rather independent animal, it might obey you only when it sees fit to do so.

Before meals is an excellent time to teach a kitten a skill, as dinner proves a suitable reward. As for "household commands"—"No," "Down" and others—your kitten will learn these and obey them if you really mean business. Constant repetition of the commands and an occasional spank on the rump will help the kitten to learn not to jump on tables and other places where it is not wanted.

COMING WHEN CALLED

Any kitten or cat can easily be trained to come when you call. Choose a name for your pet and start using the name as soon as you get the kitten. One of the best ways to condition it to respond to its name is by starting to call the kitten to its meals. Gradually, it will respond to its name wherever it is, indoors or outdoors.

LEASH TRAINING

Kittens and cats must have fresh air and sunshine. If you live in an apartment or a house in a city where you can't let your kitten run loose, leash-training is important. If you have a female cat which you don't want roaming the neighborhood "husband hunting," leash-training is very important. The training, too, will prove a boon to you when you take your cat traveling by car.

It is rumored that Siamese cats are rather easily trained to walk on a leash. This is a myth. It is true that you often see a leashed Siamese, but this is because people who own a pedigreed Siamese, or any other valuable cat for that matter, hesitate to take the risk of letting the cat roam freely. They spend more time and patience training it instead of just trying and giving up after a short period of time.

Training a cat to a leash should begin when it is still a kitten. Kittens tend to learn very quickly. First, it is best to accustom the young animal fully to the collar or, better yet, the harness (see the previous discussion on collars) by letting the kitten sniff at it and perhaps bat it around a bit. Before you put it on your pet, pick your kitten up, cuddle it and assure it that everything is fine. Show it that you are

Harnesses, collars and leashes should be part of your cat's life. Your cat should look forward to being leashed, as it signals an adventure outdoors with you, the one it loves. A Sally Anne Thompson photo.

not actually restricting its precious freedom but enabling it to see more of the world. After your kitten has become accustomed to the collar or harness for a day or two and can take it as a matter of course, snap the leash on (make sure it is lightweight) and let your kitten walk around where it wants to go. When it finds it can still meander as it pleases, then gently start it going in the direction *you* want. Most kittens and cats will fight the leash at the first authoritative tug. Your kitten may "play dead" and not walk at all, being perfectly content to let you drag it around.

A kitten or cat that resists the leash in the house may change its mind if taken outdoors. It is, however, better to start the training indoors as there is a minimum of distraction here, and your pet is on familiar ground.

A Siamese breeder in Ithaca, New York, has a queen that sits tied to the front porch and watches the cars go by. This cat also is content to be tied to a "trolley" run in the back yard (a wire strung from one tree to another, with the leash looped over it so the cat can run the length of the wire) for hours, with no danger of straying into other people's yards or onto the road.

SITTING UP

Almost any kitten can learn to sit up for its dinner, if the dinner is held within reach above the kitten's head and the words "Sit up" are repeated. The kitten's natural impulse *is* to reach up for it, and soon your pet will associate the words with the deed and sit up on command any time.

RETRIEVING

An English authority on cats had only one cat that would retrieve. If she threw a wooden ball, the cat would bring it back to be thrown again. This cat was a "natural" retriever, her mistress wrote.

I had one cat that would retrieve small sticks. Frisky was a neutered shorthair, about six months old. At the time, I was teaching Tammy, a collie pup, to retrieve and since the dog proved slow to learn, Frisky would bring me a stick to throw. I'd toss it, and then he'd patiently try to teach Tammy. Or when I'd throw a stick to Tammy, and he would just sit there and look at me, the cat would finally go and get it and show it to Tammy. He never did manage to teach the dog, but he had a lot of fun and got a lot of exercise in the attempt.

A friend of mine has a Siamese neuter a year old that retrieves, but he does it only in the wee hours of the morning!

SHAKING HANDS

You can try teaching your kitten to "shake hands," but most cats seem to consider it beneath their dignity. It may

Almost any kitten can learn to sit up, especially if you hold a bit of its favorite food just out of reach. Your pet shop will have a special book on cat training which will teach you how to train your cat. Photo by Dr. H. R. Axelrod.

be that they realize what you expect, but that dosen't change matters.

ROLLING OVER

Some kittens can be trained to roll over. Since a kitten will roll over instinctively if you tickle its stomach, you can keep repeating "Roll over" and tickling it when it does. The kitten will eventually get the idea. Remember that kittens and cats like to be scratched but only when they, not you, desire it.

OTHER TRICKS

Your kitten's (or cat's) natural tricks and games (those they learn themselves, by copying what you do or by sheer inventiveness) are just as good or even better than what you can teach them to do. Kittens especially can keep you amused for hours, as they run and scamper, and pounce on imaginary mice.

Some kittens and cats are born actors. They'll run and play around the house, but when visitors come in, they'll *really* put on a show: running, mewing for attention, being underfoot, or by showing off some of the tricks you had given up trying to teach.

Then there are the shy cats—you've taught them tricks and bragged about them. When friends stop by you can't even find the beasts and if you do, they act as though you are totally insane and make it appear that this whole "trick" business is something you've just made up. Remember that each cat has its own personality and that no two cats are alike.

My own cats have several self-taught tricks. Pandora takes the latch off the door when she wants to go out. All of my house cats have learned to sit on the windowsill by their feeding area when they think it's time for a meal. If they are outdoors and want to come in, they jump up and stare through the windows at me, following me from the sills as I go from room to room.

Their favorite "trick" is turning the bedroom light off and on. (They are the utility company's best customers!) Since this particular light is near the foot of the bed, for convenience I attached a cord to it so I could turn it off from the head of the bed. Sometimes the cats, singly or in groups, leap up and down for hours, turning the light on and off. If I am reading in bed at night, they turn off the light when they feel it is time for me to go to sleep.

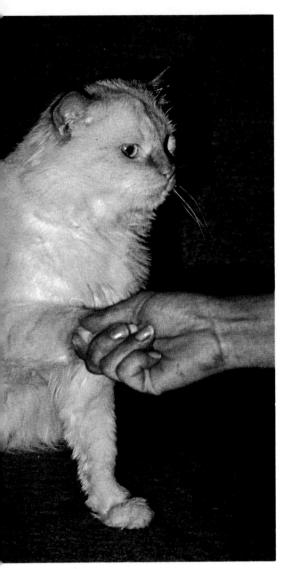

Training a cat to shake hands is very difficult, and only a well-trained cat can do it. Cats are, as a rule, difficult to train. But you can make it look as if your cat is trained by taking advantage of any special habits your particular cat might have.

Some cats are very trainable. This lovely longhair was easily trained to jump through a hoop and performed the trick every time the hoop was brought out. She jumped about four feet into the air for this stunt. Photos on this page and facing page by Dr. H. R. Axelrod.

These cats seem to be balancing a ball in the air, holding the ball outright in their claws and walking on two feet. These are, however, only trick photographs.

Health

Cats are healthy, hardy animals, but like us, they can at times get sick or have an accident. Never, never diagnose a disease yourself. A veterinarian is an experienced and knowledgeable individual—take advantage of his expertise.

As soon as you acquire a kitten (or cat), bring it to your veterinarian for a medical check-up. Your kitten will have to have inoculations for panleukopenia, the most feared of any cat disease, and for rabies and several respiratory diseases. The vet will tell you when the shots must be given. The vet will check your kitten for mites and worms, and if your pet is so afflicted the vet will give you medicine to administer to the kitten to correct the situation.

If your kitten never goes outdoors except on a leash, have the vet show you how to clip its claws. This will save your furniture and your skin. If your kitten goes out alone, don't have its claws clipped, as they are its main protection against enemies.

A cat does not mind heat and cold. Summer warmth and a frolic in the snow can both be enjoyed without difficulty. Drafts and sudden changes in temperature, however, should be avoided.

A well-balanced diet and a vitamin-mineral supplement are both important for maintaining the good health of your pet (see the chapter on feeding for a complete discussion of vitamin-mineral supplements and diet).

GIVING MEDICINES

Medicating a cat is not really very difficult to do. Your vet can show you the easiest way. Many medicines may be mixed in with the food or with milk. To give pills that cannot be ground up and mixed with food, elevate the cat's head and force the mouth open; drop the pill down the center of the mouth (over the tongue) as far back as possible. Hold the jaws closed until the cat has swallowed.

Liquid medicine is best given with an eyedropper, preferably one made of hard rubber or polyethylene (soft) plastic. (If a cat chomps down on a glass eyedropper, the results may be disastrous.)

Some cats accept medicine with little or no difficulty. Other cats may have to be wrapped and held in a towel before they'll accept it.

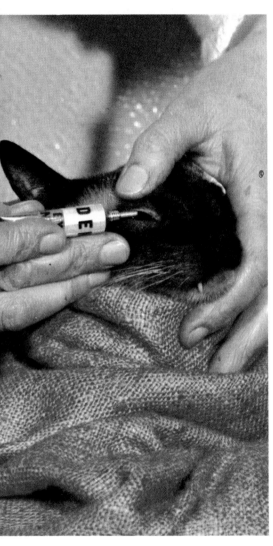

Learn how to treat your cat should it become ill or injured. The first lesson is to wrap the cat up in a heavy towel or cloth so it can't scratch you, jump away or struggle for freedom. Then apply the treatment. Photo by Sally Anne Thompson.

FLEAS

Some cats that stay in the house all the time are lucky enough not to have any fleas, ever. Many cats that go outdoors, however, often come home with fleas. You can buy either a commercial flea powder or spray or have your vet recommend one. Make sure that you buy a product that has been formulated for use on cats. Never use products made for dogs. Follow carefully the directions given on the package when applying the flea treatment. You do not want to get any in the cat's eyes, ears, nose or mouth.

RINGWORM

Cats rarely get ringworm, a fungus disease that is hard to detect and which is very contagious and can pass from man to animal and from animal to man. The cat will be scratching itself and there will be a rough spot on the cat's coat, with the hair around it dry and breaking off, and the skin discolored. If you suspect your cat has ringworm, take it to your veterinarian for diagnosis and treatment.

MITES

Mites are tiny little pests. Ear mites, a quite common kind, thrive in cats' ears, causing a dark discharge, reddened skin, itching and discomfort. This must be treated by a veterinarian. Do not treat any ear ailment at home, except under the instruction of a vet.

MANGE

Mange must be diagnosed and treated by a veterinarian. General symptoms include falling or rough and dry hair; scaly skin; blisters; a scratching cat and discolored skin. Mange is caused by mange mites. It is communicable and spreads rapidly all over one cat and then to others.

If you suspect your cat has mange, isolate the animal until you can take it to your vet, which should be as soon as possible. The danger of transmitting the condition is very great. Wash your hands thoroughly after you touch any cat you think might have mange.

ECZEMA

Eczema looks similar to mange, but it is neither parasitic nor contagious. It stems from improper feeding, dirt and dampness. Your vet will diagnose it and tell you how to treat it.

TICKS

Ticks are the most gruesome of the external parasites. They desensitize the skin of their victims so they can bury their heads in the skin and suck blood. Their bodies remain

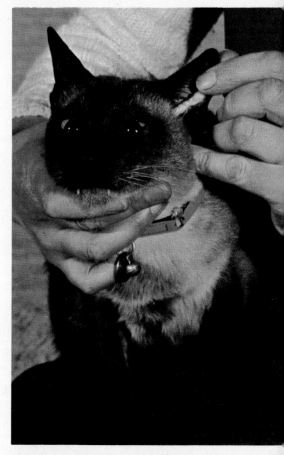

Never treat your cat's ears by yourself. Certainly never force any kind of probe into your cat's ears unless you are directed to do so by a veterinarian. Photo by Sally Anne Thompson.

This beautiful Siamese may be having fun in the sun, but it can also be picking up fleas and ticks at the same time. A good flea collar will usually take care of these parasites, but be sure to change the flea collar regularly.

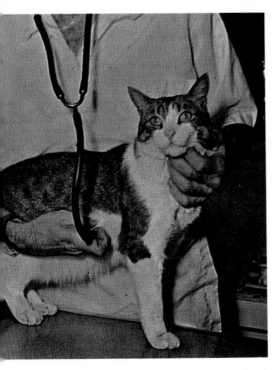

outside, swelling up with blood into large, reddish brown blobs, which are easily recognized.

To get rid of these, the ticks must first be killed and *then* lifted off the animal with tweezers. (If a tick is simply pulled off, the head will remain in the skin.) There are several commercial products which you can use to kill ticks, but make sure that the product you purchase is formulated for cats.

If your cat goes outdoors a lot, check it over when it comes in the house during the "tick season" (spring, summer, early fall). Ticks can cause a fever and blood poisoning.

WORMS

Roundworms, the most common worms found in cats, are long and round and are generally expelled coiled. They are white and ugly. Tapeworms are excreted in small segments resembling small brown grains of rice. Your cat may drag its hind end along the floor to ease the itching and discomfort caused by worms. The cat may eat more than usual and it may have alternating diarrhea and constipation.

Worms are frequent in kittens but not in all kittens. If your kitten or cat has worms, it may be sluggish, its coat will be dull, it will be thin but its stomach will protrude and its breath will have a sickishly sweet odor. You may see worms in the feces or vomitus.

Do not treat worms yourself. Your veterinarian should be given a sample of your kitten's stool which he will examine to determine what kind of worms (if any) it has. He will then worm the cat accordingly.

VOMITING

If your cat throws its dinner up once, don't worry. The food may have been the wrong temperature, or the cat may not have chewed the food thoroughly. If your pet throws up more than once, watch closely for other symptoms. If you find hair or felt-like balls or strips in the vomitus, your cat has hair balls. If the vomitus is oddly colored, frothy, odoriferous or bloody, bring the cat and a sample of the vomitus to your vet for examination.

HAIR BALLS

Hair balls are the result of too little grooming. All the loose hairs cats lick off during their "baths" go into their stomachs where they pile up. Long-haired cats are more subject to this and need more grooming.

Some people believe that a little vegetable oil, butter or pure salad oil given at room temperature will help your cat pass these. Never give your cat castor oil, as it is too strong, and never give mineral oil because it absorbs vitamins from

Above: Have your cat checked regularly by your local veterinarian. Below: The cat's habit of cleaning itself often results in hair balls forming in the stomach. Left: A healthy cat is one that is well cared for.

food and retards digestion. If there is a severe blockage, the vet should be consulted.

With regular careful grooming of your cat, you can help to prevent hair balls.

CONSTIPATION

Constipation may be caused by hair balls. It may also be caused by improper feeding or insufficient exercise. Make sure your pet gets more exercise, and add some roughage or a little liver to your cat's diet; this should relieve the constipation. Never give a cat a laxative or an enema. If there is no noticeable improvement after several days, consult your veterinarian.

FOREIGN OBJECTS

If your cat has something caught in its throat, it will cough and paw at its throat and neck. Cover the cat with a large towel so it won't thrash about, and then look in its mouth (you may need two people for this; one person can hold the cat while the other one looks in the mouth). Never try to take bones or other foreign objects out of your cat's throat yourself unless the foreign object is dull-sided, you can see it at the top of the throat and it has not broken the skin. It may be possible that such objects may be removed with your fingers or with tweezers. If you do not see anything or if you see something sharp, rush the cat to your veterinarian immediately!

If your pet has swallowed foreign matter, give it some soft bulky food such as bread soaked with water, or give it plain warm water. Then, after it has eaten or drunk as much as possible, put a bit of salt on the back of its tongue to bring up the matter. If it isn't regurgitated and you *know* the cat has swallowed something, watch your pet closely. If its stomach protrudes, if it vomits or if it develops diarrhea, take it to the vet.

If your cat has swallowed string, do not attempt to pull out the string. Cut it off at the mouth, and if the remainder is not passed within a day, consult the vet.

DIARRHEA

Diarrhea is often caused by incorrect feeding or eating new foods. If incorrect feeding is the cause, withhold food for about twelve hours. New foods should always be introduced gradually in order to avoid upsets to the cat's system. If milk seems to be the cause of diarrhea (and this might be especially true for a kitten), reduce the amount of milk offered or eliminate it from your pet's diet.

Diarrhea can also be a symptom of a more serious disorder. If it continues for more than a reasonable length of time, consult your veterinarian.

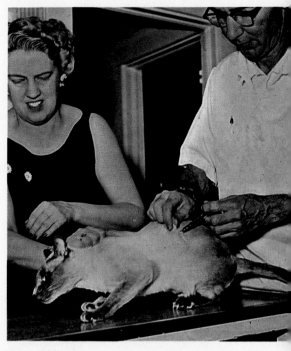

Your veterinarian can, and usually will, suggest that your cat be immunized against a variety of illnesses including the dreaded panleukopenia (feline distemper).

A magnificent white Persian kitten.

52

A lovely sealpoint Himalayan kitten.

If your kitten or cat is suffering from diarrhea, whatever the cause, keep the animal warm and have it rest as much as possible.

PANLEUKOPENIA

Panleukopenia, sometimes called feline infectious enteritis or feline distemper, is fast-moving, horrible and fatal. This is not the same disease as distemper in dogs. It is a disease of cats and cats only. It can strike any cat anywhere, as germs are carried in the air, on the bottom of shoes, on hands and in many other ways. Since no cure will work unreservedly, an ounce of prevention is most assuredly worth a pound of cure.

In order to protect your kitten from this disease, it should be inoculated when it is about three months old. Two inoculations are given, about ten days apart. They produce no aftereffects, and your kitten will then be safe the rest of its life. If a kitten younger than this is exposed to the disease, the vet can give it a temporary shot of serum which is effective for ten days.

A small kitten may die of the disease before it shows any signs of the illness. The general symptoms are refusal to eat, fever, vomiting, runny eyes, poor coat and general malaise. The animal becomes dehydrated and eventually it isn't able to stand up. A cat suspected of enteritis cannot be hospitalized because the disease is too contagious. If you suspect the disease, call the vet immediately and have him come to your home. Speed is very important because death may occur in twenty-four hours.

If there is an epidemic in your area, have your vet give your inoculated cats booster shots and your kittens temporary shots.

If you have had an infected cat, wait about five or six months before bringing a new kitten or cat into the house. Burn all of the former cat's bedding, brushes and other things used by the cat, and disinfect the house thoroughly.

HEAT PROSTRATION

Heat prostration is most prevalent in old cats, overweight cats and very young kittens. Unless the area is well shaded, never play with your pet in very hot weather and surely not in direct sunlight. Cats will avoid too much direct heat from the sun and too much exercise in the heat, if they can. If your cat collapses, bring it indoors, gently massage it and put some ice on the back of its head and neck. If the cat is not unconscious, give it water in which a bit of sugar has been mixed. Keep the animal quiet. If improvement does not occur within an hour, call your veterinarian.

Kittens have a natural tendency to claw anything small that moves quickly.

RUNNY EYES

If your pet's eyes get red and runny and the area around the eyes swells, it may have conjunctivitis, or it may have a cold, pneumonia or pneumonitis. A local irritation caused by a hair or speck of dirt may also cause this condition.

The only safe treatment at home for a kitten's or cat's eyes is flushing them out with a warm, mild boric acid solution. Bathe the eyes frequently. If, in a day to two, you do not notice a change for the better, call your veterinarian.

COLDS

When a cat has a cold, it must be kept warm and dry, and fed light but nourishing liquids. You may bathe its eyes with boric acid solution and gently wipe its nose with a moist tissue. Keep feeding it a balanced diet, along with increased liquids and a vitamin-mineral supplement, to keep up its strength. If in forty-eight hours you notice either no change or a change for the worse, call your veterinarian.

RABIES

Every kitten should be vaccinated against rabies before it is six months old, and every cat should be revaccinated every year. If your cat is bitten by a rabid dog, bat or squirrel it may become violent, biting and scratching, and is certainly dangerous. Wrap the cat up in a towel or put it in a *closed* basket, and take it to your veterinarian immediately.

POISONING

You should, of course, keep household cleaners and disinfectants and any other things that might be poisonous to your pet in a closed cupboard or closet. If your pet *has* swallowed poison or if you think it has, get a vet immediately. If you know what the poison was, tell the vet on the phone and he will instruct you in proper first-aid measures.

SNAKE BITE

If poisonous snakes live in your area of the country, you should have anti-venom serum on hand at all times. If your cat should be bitten by a snake, administer snake bite serum as directed on the package. Slashing the wound (so that the blood will flow freely and carry away the poison) and washing the wound in tepid running water will also help. If the bite is on a leg, apply a tourniquet above the wound. Take the cat to the vet after these first-aid measures have been taken.

CUTS AND SCRATCHES

If your kitten or cat gets cut, whether by broken glass, the sharp edge of an opened can or the teeth of another animal,

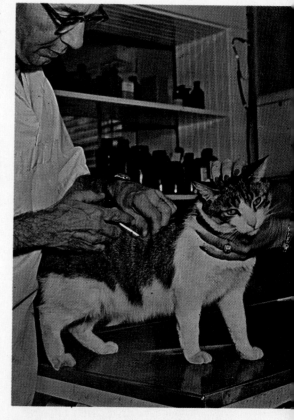

Every kitten should be vaccinated against rabies before it is six months old; as it grows older, it should be revaccinated every year.

Long-haired kittens. On the top is a lovely pair of cream longhairs; the two in the lower left photo are tabbies, while the single kitten is a silver. These kittens have not yet attained the mature coloration of their eyes.

wash the cut well with soap and running water. Unless a vein or artery is slashed, let the wound bleed freely for a minute or two, to flush out some of the dirt and germs. Apply an antiseptic and wrap the cut firmly with gauze. The dressing will probably have to be replaced frequently because the cat will remove it.

If the cut is very deep, clip the fur around it. If the cut is bleeding profusely, the first thing to do is to stop the flow of blood by holding gauze on the wound and applying pressure. If the cut is on a leg, use a tourniquet between the cut and cat's heart. Release the pressure on the tourniquet every three to five minutes. Rush the cat to the veterinarian.

BURNS

If the burn is a slight one, apply a dressing saturated with a mild tea or baking soda solution to the affected part. If a large area of the cat was burned, cool the burn with cold water, cover all of the burned section with a tea solution and take the cat to the veterinarian. A cat with a bad burn may suffer from shock and should be kept warm and quiet.

The same applies to scalds.

BROKEN BONES AND FALLS

If your cat breaks a bone, it should be set by a veterinarian immediately. If you suspect a broken bone, handle the cat as little and as gently as possible and take it to your vet.

Your cat's collar should be changed frequently, as it can wear out and fall off the cat while it scrambles through bushes. Your name and telephone number should be inscribed on a tag, or inserted in a small container, which is then attached to the collar.

Two cute Himalayan kittens. Photo by Fritz Prenzel.

If the cat has fallen but shows no symptoms of broken bones, it is possible that there may be internal injuries. Pale gums, rapid and weak pulse or bleeding from the nose, mouth or rectum or blood in the urine may indicate internal bleeding. Keep the animal as quiet as possible, handle the cat gently and get to the vet immediately.

RICKETS

Your kitten should never be troubled by rickets. If it is, the fault is probably due to improper feeding which is the major cause of this crippling disease. A cat with rickets is characterized by bowed legs, enlarged joints, irregular teeth and a lack of energy. To prevent rickets and its accompanying malformations, kittens should be fed a good balanced diet and a vitamin-mineral supplement so that you can be sure of fulfilling their nutritional needs.

TEETH AND GUM PROBLEMS

Kittens chew and gnaw while they are teething. They also chew and gnaw for the fun of it. Your kitten should have no trouble shedding its milk teeth for firm adult teeth. Cats swallow their teeth—it's perfectly normal.

Older cats sometimes have a build-up of tartar on their teeth or have toothaches, as their teeth decay with time. If your cat doesn't eat well, has trouble chewing or continually paws its face and shakes its head, look inside its mouth. If there is discoloration of the gums or signs of abcesses, take the cat to the vet who will take appropriate action. Scaling (removing excess tartar) and tooth extraction are jobs for your vet.

**Above: A pair of blue longhairs.
Below: A pair of tabby longhairs
and a single black long-haired
kitten.**

Showing Your Cat

Any cat at all can be shown! This will surprise you if you thought that only the "aristocats" of felinity were eligible. Most cat shows have well over one hundred classes, so there is room for one and all—even your household pet.

THE "DANGERS" OF SHOWING

The dangers of showing are often discussed. Non-showers are forever harping on the dangers of showing. Granted, there is a risk—but the great pleasures and thrills you get are experiences which more than compensate for the minor everyday hazards.

Disease is the first danger that comes to mind. How valid is the danger? A cat that has had a contagious disease or that has had recent contact with a diseased cat cannot—and should not—be shown. All the clubs have stiff penalties against members showing diseased animals. Remember, too, a sick cat is never at its best.

The rules governing health and sanitation at shows sponsored by recognized and reputable cat associations are very specific; they are enforced for your cat's best protection and well-being, and you should respect them in that light. Some cat associations require the presence of a veterinarian at every one of their cat shows. You could be asked to attach a "note from the doctor" with your entry blank—the written certification from your vet that your cat is in the pink! In other show situations, the show manager or an official of the show committee or even a judge may suspect the "funny look" of a particular animal and the owner or exhibitor will be immediately required to have his cat undergo veterinary inspection.

As for the psychological dangers of a show for your cat, most cats and kittens are unaffected. To be sure, a house cat may not like a cage, but your love and the cat's natural curiosity help it to take it in its stride. A very shy cat may strenuously object to being shown in a cage, but the cages are roomy and most cats are either born showmen or simply sleep through the whole show!

The advantages of shows are many: they help to uphold the various breeds' standards; they enable you to compare your cats with the very best in catdom; you can get an honest evaluation of your cat (whether you should use your cat for breeding or not) if you have a pure-bred and how it stands up to the others; you meet similarly-minded folk and have a chance to discuss cats and related problems to your heart's content—and last but not least, the ribbons! Nothing is quite

This silver Persian is sometimes called a "Chinchilla" because of its beautiful coat.

as much of an ego-booster as a pretty rosette, or a silky ribbon, and the pride of ownership that accompanies it!

So you have decided to show! Wonderful! Now your major problem is to find a show!

HOW TO FIND A SHOW

Any of the major organizations will gladly tell you of an affiliated club in your area; shows are advertised in the newspapers; many of the cat specialty magazines carry the notices; a breeder in the area will help you; even some pet stores have show information.

When you have located a show, write to the club secretary and request a copy of show rules of the sponsoring organization, entry blanks and the "specials" (closing date for entries, list of classes, fees, time and so forth). Generally the closing date for entries is approximately one month before the date of the show.

The fees depend upon the size of the show, how many classes you are entering your cat in and whether the cat is registered with the sponsoring organization. If your animal is not registered, a listing fee to list your cat with the show manager must be paid. House pets, neuters and spays are very often excepted from this listing. Fees for a cat show are usually very reasonable.

ENTRY BLANKS

On the entry blank you will usually be asked to fill in the following information: breed; color; sex; eye color; registration number, or listing; name; birth date; breeder (if the owner of your cat's dam is not known to you, just write "unknown"); sire and dam (either their names or "unknown"); agent (if you are shipping your cat or sending it with someone else); your name and address; the numbers of the classes in which your cat is to be entered; and perhaps a health statement to be completed by your veterinarian.

After you have returned the entry blank and fee to the show manager, you will be sent an acknowledgment. Save this, as some shows require it at show time.

GETTING READY FOR THE SHOW

Getting your cat into "show shape" should not be difficult since your cat should already be in good condition because you've been providing a good balanced diet and a vitamin-mineral supplement and you've been grooming it every day. Just before the show, take extra time to groom your cat carefully and make sure there is a real shine to its coat.

Check the show rules for the equipment you must bring to the show. You might need a blanket (to put in the bottom of the pen) and a litter pan and water bowl of a particular

Many show groomers have special "tricks" such as sprinkling talcum powder into the coat and working it down into the roots of the fur. Then they brush and comb it out. Photo by Sally Anne Thompson.

Facing page: A nice pair of brown tabby longhairs.

A champion Siamese with some of her ribbons. Cat shows are great places to meet nice people whose interests in cats might well be similar to your own.

color. Bring your own litter and some of your cat's favorite food. Any other equipment that you think you might need such as grooming combs or brushes should be gathered together ahead of time so that you don't forget anything on the big day.

When the big day has arrived, plan to get to the show a little early so you can find your assigned number. If there is a veterinarian present, he will need time to check all the entrants as soon as they arrive. Once these routines are out of the way, you can put your cat in its pen or cage. Comfort it a while; inspect its appearance. You can also make use of your time to view your competition and make new friends.

THE JUDGING

The judge will pick up your cat and examine it closely. Coloring, body and tail, general proportions and conformation, head and ears, eyes, coat and condition are all taken into consideration. The house pet class, which you may be entered in, is judged solely on beauty and condition. The judge may look at your cat once or several times. Your cat may stay in the judging cage a while or may be returned immediately. If your animal is returned, don't feel badly. Yours probably won't be the only one returned. Generally, as you compare your cat with others, you will be able to see your animal's good and bad points, but if you have questions, most judges will be glad to talk with you after all the judging has been completed.

The golden rule in cat showing is: never be a poor loser. Congratulate the winners as you would like to have been congratulated. If the judge feels it is worth your while, try again at another show.

Don't give up on the first try, unless a judge (and judges' opinions vary too!) advises you to get better stock. Remember, your household pet class observes no standards other than beauty and condition—one judge's ideas may differ radically from those of another!

No one may leave the show until the judging is over, unless granted special permission.

When you get your cat home, watch it closely for a week or two. If it gets runny eyes or diarrhea, or you notice some other condition that is not normal, call your veterinarian. Tell him the animal has been shown and be prompt in reporting any symptoms. If your cat has picked up any ailment, the vet may be able to cure it before your pet becomes seriously ill. Generally, you won't have to worry, as all possible precautions against disease are taken at a cat show.

One reason that cats are as popular as they are is that they are among the most beautiful and gracefully appealing of all animals, as the kitten at left amply demonstrates.

SOME CAT STANDARDS

The following are representative samples of standards for just a few of the cat breeds recognized in the United States. These standards are those of the Cat Fanciers' Association and are printed directly from *CFA Show Standards*, which contains the standards for all of the recognized cat breeds. The complete book of standards is available from the Cat Fanciers' Association, Inc. (1309 Allaire Avenue, Ocean, NJ 07712) and costs only $1.50.

BURMESE

POINT SCORE

HEAD (25)
Roundness of Head 7
Breadth between eyes 4
Full Face with Proper Profile 8
Ear Set and Placement 6

EYES (5)
Placement and shape 5

BODY (30)
Torso 15
Muscle Tone 5
Legs and Feet 5
Tail 5

COAT (10)
Short 4
Texture 4
Close Lying 2

COLOR (30)
Body Color 25
Eye Color 5

GENERAL: The overall impression of the ideal Burmese would be a cat of medium size and rich solid color; with substantial bone structure, good muscular development and a surprising weight for its size. This, together with its expressive eyes and sweet face, presents a totally distinctive cat which is comparable to no other breed. Perfect physical condition, with excellent muscle tone. There should be no evidence of obesity, paunchiness, weakness, or apathy.

HEAD: Pleasingly rounded without flat planes whether viewed from front or side. Face full, with considerable breadth between the eyes, tapering slightly to a short, well developed muzzle. In profile there should be a visible nose break.

EARS: Medium in size and set well apart on a rounded skull; alert, tilting slightly forward, broad at base with slightly rounded tips.

EYES: Set far apart and with rounded aperture.

BODY: Medium in size, muscular in development, and presenting a compact appearance. Allowance to be made for larger size in males. An ample, rounded chest, with back level from shoulder to tail.

LEGS: Well proportioned to body.

PAWS: Round. Toes, five in front and four behind.

TAIL: Straight, medium in length.

COAT: Fine, glossy, satin-like in texture; short and close lying.

COLOR: The mature specimen should be rich, warm **sable brown**; shading almost imperceptibly to a slightly lighter hue on the underparts, but otherwise without shadings or markings of any kind. Nose Leather: Brown. Paw Pads: Brown. Eye Color: Ranging from yellow to gold, the greater the depth and brilliance the better.

PENALIZE: Green Eyes.

DISQUALIFY: Kinked or abnormal tail. Locket or button. Incorrect number of toes. Blue Eyes.

ABYSSINIAN

GENERAL: The overall impression of the ideal Abyssinian would be a colorful cat of medium size giving the impression of eager activity and showing a lively interest in all surroundings. Lithe, hard and muscular. Sound health and general vigor. Well balanced temperamentally and physically; gentle and amenable to handling.

HEAD: A modified, slightly rounded wedge without flat planes; the brow, cheek and profile lines all showing a gentle contour. A slight rise from the bridge of the nose to the forehead, which should be of good size with width between the ears and flowing into the arched neck without a break.

MUZZLE: Not sharply pointed or square. The chin should be neither receding nor protruding. Allowance should be made for jowls in adult males.

EARS: Alert, large, and moderately pointed; broad, and cupped at base and set as though listening. Hair on ears very short and close-lying, preferably tipped with black or dark brown on a ruddy Abyssinian or chocolate brown on a red Abyssinian.

EYES: Almond-shaped, large, brilliant and expressive. Neither round nor Oriental. Eyes accentuated by dark lidskin, encircled by light-colored area.

BODY: Medium long, lithe and graceful, but showing well-developed muscular strength without coarseness. Abyssinian conformation strikes a medium between the extremes of the cobby and the svelte lengthy type. Proportion and general balance more to be desired than mere size.

LEGS AND FEET: Proportionately slim, fine boned. The Abyssinian stands well off the ground giving the impression of being on tip toe. Paws small, oval, and compact. Toes, five in front and four behind.

PAWS: Small, oval and compact. When standing, giving the impression of being on tiptoe. Toes, five in front and four behind.

TAIL: Thick at base, fairly long and tapering.

COAT: Soft, silky, fine in texture, but dense and resilient to the touch with a lustrous sheen. Medium in length but long enough to accomodate two or three bands of ticking.

PENALIZE: Off-Color pads. Long narrow head. Short round head. Barring on legs. Rings on tail. Coldness or grey tones in coat.

DISQUALIFY: White locket, or white anywhere other than nostril, chin and upper throat area. Kinked or abnormal tail. Dark unbroken necklace. Grey undercoat close to the skin extending throughout a major portion of the body. Any black hair on red Abyssinian. Incorrect number of toes.

ABYSSINIAN COLORS

RUDDY: Coat ruddy brown, ticked with various shades of darker brown or black; the extreme outer tip to be the darkest, with orange-brown undercoat, ruddy to the skin. Darker shading along spine allowed if fully ticked. Tail tipped with black and without rings. The undersides and forelegs (inside) to be a tint to harmonize with the main color. Preference given to UNMARKED orange-brown (burnt-sienna) color. Nose Leather: Tile Red. Paw Pads: Black or brown, with black between toes and extending slightly beyond the paws. Eye Color: Gold or green, the more richness and depth of color the better.

RED: Warm, glowing red, distinctly ticked with chocolate-brown. Deeper shades of red preferred. However, good ticking not to be sacrificed merely for depth of color. Ears and tail tipped with chocolate-brown. Nose Leather: Rosy pink. Paw Pads: Pink, with chocolate-brown between toes, extending slightly beyond paws. Eye Color: Gold or green, the more richness and depth of color the better.

AMERICAN SHORTHAIR

GENERAL: The American Shorthair is believed by some naturalists to be the original breed of domestic cat. It has for many, many centuries adapted itself willingly and cheerfully to the needs of man, but without allowing itself to become effete or its natural intelligence to diminish. Its disposition and habits are exemplary as a house pet, a pet and companion for children, but the feral instinct lies not too far beneath the surface and this breed of cat remains capable of self-sufficiency when the need arises. Its hunting instinct is so strong that it exercises the skill even when well provided with food. This is our only breed of true "working cat." The conformation of the breed is well adapted for this and reflects its refusal to surrender its natural functions. This is a cat lithe enough to stalk its prey, but powerful enough to make the kill easily. Its reflexes are under perfect control. Its legs are long enough to cope with any terrain and heavy and muscular enough for high leaps. The face is long enough to permit easy grasping by the teeth with jaws so powerful they can close against resistance. Its coat is dense enough to protect from moisture, cold and superficial skin injuries, but short enough and of sufficiently hard texture to resist matting or entanglement when slipping through heavy vegetation. No part of the anatomy is so exaggerated as to foster weakness. The general effect is that of the trained athlete, with all muscles rippling easily beneath the skin, the flesh lean and hard, and with great latent power held in reserve.

HEAD: Large, with full-cheeked face giving the impression of an oblong just slightly longer than wide.

NECK: Medium in length, muscular and strong.

NOSE: Medium in length, same width for entire length, with a gentle curve.

MUZZLE: Squared. Definite jowls in studs.

CHIN: Firm and well-developed, forming perpendicular line with upper lip.

EARS: Medium, slightly rounded at tips, set wide and not unduly open at base.

EYES: Round and wide with slight slant to outer aperture. Set well apart. Bright, clear and alert.

BODY: Medium to large, well-knit, powerful and hard with well-developed chest and heavy shoulders. No sacrifice of quality for the sake of mere size.

LEGS: Medium in length, firm-boned and heavily muscled, showing capability for easy jumping.

PAWS: Firm, full and rounded, with heavy pads. Toes: five in front, four behind.

TAIL: Medium long, heavy at base, tapering to an abrupt blunt end in appearance, but with normal tapering final vertebrae.

COAT: Short, thick, even and hard in texture. Somewhat heavier and thicker during the winter months.

PENALIZE: Excessive cobbiness or ranginess. Very short tail. Obesity or boniness.

DISQUALIFY: Deep nose break. Long or fluffy fur. Kinked or abnormal tail. Locket or button. Any appearance of hybridization with any other breed. Incorrect number of toes.

AMERICAN SHORTHAIR COLORS

WHITE: Pure glistening white. Nose Leather: Pink. Paw Pads: Pink. Eye Color: Deep blue or brilliant gold. Odd-eyed whites shall have one blue and one gold eye with equal color depth.

BLACK: Dense coal black, sound from roots to tip of fur. Free from any tinge of rust on tips or smoke undercoat. Nose Leather: Black. Paw Pads: Black or brown. Eye Color: Brilliant gold.

BLUE: Blue, lighter shade preferred, one level tone from nose to tip of tail. Sound to the roots. A sound darker shade is more acceptable than an unsound lighter shade. Nose Leather: Blue. Paw Pads: Blue. Eye Color: Brilliant gold.

RED: Deep, rich, clear, brilliant red; without shading, markings, or ticking. Lips and chin the same color as coat. Nose Leather: Brick Red. Paw Pads: Brick Red. Eye Color: Brilliant Gold.

CREAM: One Level Shade of buff cream, without markings. Sound to the roots. Lighter shades preferred. Nose Leather: Pink. Paw Pads: Pink. Eye Color: Brilliant Gold.

CHINCHILLA: Undercoat pure white. Coat on back, flanks, head and tail sufficiently tipped with black to give the characteristic sparkling silver appearance. Legs may be slightly shaded with tipping. Chin and ear tufts, stomach and chest, pure white. Rims of eyes, lips and nose outlined with black. Nose Leather: Brick Red. Paw Pads: Black. Eye Color: Green or Blue-Green.

SHADED SILVER: Undercoat white with a mantle of black tipping shading down from sides, face and tail from dark on the ridge to white on the chin, chest, stomach and under the tail. Legs to be the same tone as the face. The general effect to be much darker than a chinchilla. Rims of eyes, lips and nose outlined with black. Nose Leather: Brick Red. Paw Pads: Black. Eye Color: Green or Blue-Green.

SHELL CAMEO (Red Chinchilla): Undercoat white, the coat on the back, flanks, head and tail to be sufficiently tipped with red to give the characteristic sparkling appearance. Face and legs may be very slightly shaded with tipping. Chin, ear tufts, stomach and chest white. Nose Leather: Rose. Rims of Eyes: Rose. Paw Pads: Rose. Eye Color: Brilliant Gold.

SHADED CAMEO (Red Shaded): Undercoat white with a mantle of red tipping shading down the sides, face, and tail from dark on the ridge to white on the chin, chest, stomach, and under the tail. Legs to be the same tone as face. The general effect to be much redder than the Shell Cameo. Nose Leather: Rose. Rims of Eyes: Rose. Paw Pads: Rose. Eye Color: Brilliant Gold.

BLACK SMOKE: White undercoat, deeply tipped with black. Cat in repose appears black. In motion the white undercoat is clearly apparent. Points and mask black with narrow band of white at base of hairs next to skin which may be seen only when the fur is parted. Nose Leather: Black. Paw Pads: Black. Eye Color: Brilliant Gold.

BLUE SMOKE: White undercoat, deeply tipped with blue. Cat in repose appears blue. In motion the white undercoat is clearly apparent. Points and mask blue, with narrow band of white at base of hairs next to skin which may be seen only when fur is parted. Nose Leather: Blue. Paw Pads: Blue. Eye Color: Brilliant Gold.

CAMEO SMOKE (Red Smoke): White undercoat, deeply tipped with red. Cat in repose appears red. In motion the white undercoat is clearly apparent. Points and mask red with narrow band of white at base of hairs next to skin, which may be seen only when fur is parted. Nose Leather: Rose. Rims of Eyes: Rose. Paw Pads: Rose. Eye Color: Brilliant Gold.

TORTOISESHELL SMOKE: White undercoat deeply tipped with black with clearly defined, unbrindled patches of red and cream tipped hairs as in the pattern of the Tortoiseshell. Cat in repose appears Tortoiseshell. In motion, the white undercoat is clearly apparent. Face and ears Tortoiseshell pattern with narrow band of white at the base of the hairs next to the skin that may be seen only when hair is parted. White ear tufts. Eye Color: Brilliant Gold. Blaze of red or cream tipping on face is desirable.

CLASSIC TABBY PATTERN: Markings dense, clearly defined and broad. Legs evenly barred with bracelets coming up to meet the body markings. Tail evenly ringed. Several unbroken necklaces on neck and upper chest, the more the better. Frown marks on forehead form intricate letter "M." Unbroken line runs back from outer corner of eye. Swirls on cheeks. Vertical lines over back of head extend to shoulder markings which are in the shape of a butterfly with both upper and lower wings distinctly outlined and marked with dots inside outline. Back markings consist of a vertical line down the spine from butterfly to tail with a vertical strip paralleling it on each side, the three stripes well separated by stripes of the ground color. Large solid blotch on each side to be encircled by one or more unbroken rings. Side markings should be the same on both sides. Double vertical row of buttons on chest and stomach.

MACKEREL TABBY PATTERN: Markings dense, clearly defined, and all narrow pencillings. Legs evenly barred with narrow bracelets coming up to meet the body markings. Tail Barred. Necklaces on neck and chest distinct, like so many chains. Head barred with an "M" on the forehead. Unbroken lines running back from the eyes. Lines running down the head to meet the shoulders. Spine lines run together to form a narrow saddle. Narrow pencillings run around body.

PATCHED TABBY PATTERN: A Patched Tabby (Torbie) is an established silver, brown, or blue tabby with patches of red and/or cream.

BROWN PATCHED TABBY: Ground color brilliant coppery brown with classic or mackerel tabby markings of dense black with patches of red and/or cream clearly defined on both body and extremities; a blaze of red and/or cream on the face is desirable. Lips and chin the same shade as the rings around the eyes. Eye Color: Brilliant Gold.

BLUE PATCHED TABBY: Ground color, including lips and chin, pale bluish ivory with classic or mackerel tabby markings

of very deep blue affording a good contrast with ground color. Patches of cream clearly defined on both body and extremities; a blaze of cream on the face is desirable. Warm fawn overtones of patina over the whole. Eye Color: Brilliant Gold.

SILVER PATCHED TABBY: Ground color, including lips and chin, pale silver with classic or mackerel tabby markings of dense black with patches of red and/or cream clearly defined on both body and extremities. A blaze of red and/or cream on the face is desirable. Eye Color: Brilliant Gold or Hazel.

SILVER TABBY: Ground color, including lips and chin, pale, clear silver. Markings dense black. Nose Leather: Brick Red. Paw Pads: Black. Eye Color: Green or Hazel.

RED TABBY: Ground color red. Markings deep rich red. Lips and chin red. Nose Leather: Brick Red. Paw Pads: Brick Red. Eye Color: Brilliant Gold.

BROWN TABBY: Ground color brilliant coppery brown. Markings dense black. Lips and chin the same shade as the rings around the eyes. Back of leg black from paw to heel. Nose Leather: Brick Red. Paw Pads: Black or Brown. Eye Color: Brilliant Gold.

BLUE TABBY: Ground color, including lips and chin, pale bluish ivory. Markings a very deep blue affording a good contrast with ground color. Warm fawn overtones or patina over the whole. Nose Leather: Old Rose. Paw Pads: Rose. Eye Color: Brilliant Gold.

CREAM TABBY: Ground color, including lips and chin, very pale cream. Markings of buff or cream sufficiently darker than the ground color to afford good contrast, but remaining within the dilute color range. Nose Leather: Pink. Paw Pads: Pink. Eye Color: Brilliant Gold.

CAMEO TABBY: Ground color off-white. Markings red. Nose Leather: Rose. Paw Pads: Rose. Eye Color: Brilliant Gold.

TORTOISESHELL: Black with unbrindled patches of red and cream. Patches clearly defined and well broken on both body and extremities. Blaze of red or cream on face is desirable. Eye Color: Brilliant Gold.

CALICO: White with unbrindled patches of black and red. White predominant on underparts. Eye Color: Brilliant Gold.

DILUTE CALICO: White with unbrindled patches of blue and cream. White predominant on underparts. Eye Color: Brilliant Gold.

BLUE-CREAM: Blue with patches of solid cream. Patches clearly defined and well broken on both body and extremities. Eye Color: Brilliant Gold.

BI-COLOR: White with unbrindled patches of black, or white with unbrindled patches of blue, or white with unbrindled patches of red, or white with unbrindled patches of cream. Eye Color: Gold, the more brilliant the better.

VAN BI-COLOR: Black and white, red and white, blue and white, cream and white. White cat with color confined to the extremities; head, tail, and legs. One or two small colored patches on body allowable.

VAN CALICO: White cat with unbrindled patches of black and red confined to the extremities; head, tail, and legs. One or two small colored patches on body allowable.

VAN BLUE-CREAM AND WHITE: White cat with unbrindled patches of blue and cream confined to the extremities; head, tail, and legs. One or two small colored patches on body allowable.

HIMALAYAN

Head (Including size and shape of eyes,
ear shape and set) 30
Type (Including shape, size, bone, and
length of tail) 20
Coat 10
Body Color 10
Point Color 10
Eye Color 10
Balance 5
Refinement 5

HEAD: Round and massive, with great breadth of skull. Round face with round underlying bone structure. Well set on a short, thick neck.

NOSE: Short, snub and broad. With "Break."

CHEEKS: Full.

JAWS: Broad and powerful.

CHIN: Full and well-developed.

EARS: Small, round tipped, tilted forward, and not unduly open at the base. Set far apart, and low on the head fitting into (without distorting) the rounded contour of the head.

EYES: Large, round and full. Set far apart and brilliant, giving a sweet expression to the face.

BODY: Of cobby type—low on the legs, deep in the chest, equally massive across shoulders and rump, with a short well-rounded middle piece. Large or medium in size. Quality the determining consideration rather than size.

BACK: Level.

LEGS: Short, thick and strong. Forelegs straight.

PAWS: Large, round and firm. Toes carried close, five in front and four behind.

TAIL: Short, but in proportion to body length. Carried without a curve and at an angle lower than the back.

COAT: Long and thick, standing off from the body. Of fine texture, glossy and full of life. Long all over the body, including the shoulders. The ruff immense and continuing in a deep frill between the front legs. Ear and toe tufts long. Brush very full.

COLOR: Body: Even, free of barring, with subtle shading when allowed. Allowance to be made for darker coloring on older cats. Shading should be subtle with definite contrast between points. Points: Mask, ears, legs, feet, tail dense and clearly defined. All of the same shade, and free of barring.

Mask covers entire face including whisker pads and is connected to ears by tracings. Mask should not extend over top of head. No ticking or white hairs in points.

PENALIZE: Lack of pigment in nose leather and/or paw pads in part or in total. Any resemblance to Peke-Face.

DISQUALIFY: Locket or button. Any tail abnormality. Crossed eyes. Incorrect number of toes. White toes. Eyes other than blue. Apparent weakness in hind quarters. Deformity of skull and/or mouth.

HIMALAYAN COLORS

SEAL POINT: Body even pale fawn to cream, warm in tone, shading gradually into lighter color on the stomach and chest. Points deep seal brown. Nose Leather: Same color as points. Paw Pads: Same color as points. Eye Color: Deep vivid blue.

CHOCOLATE POINT: Body ivory with no shading. Points milk-chocolate color, warm in tone. Nose Leather: Cinnamon Pink. Paw Pads: Cinnamon Pink. Eye Color: Deep vivid blue.

BLUE POINT: Body bluish white, cold in tone, shading gradually to white on stomach and chest. Points blue. Nose Leather: Slate colored. Paw Pads: Slate colored. Eye Color: Deep vivid blue.

LILAC POINT: Body glacial white with no shading. Points frosty grey with pinkish tone. Nose Leather: Lavender-Pink. Paw Pads: Lavender-Pink. Eye Color: Deep vivid blue.

FLAME (RED) POINT: Body creamy white. Points deep orange flame to deep red. Nose Leather: Flesh or Coral Pink. Paw Pads: Flesh or Coral Pink. Eye Color: Deep vivid blue.

CREAM POINT: Body creamy white with no shading. Points buff cream with no apricot. Nose Leather: Flesh pink or salmon coral. Paw Pads: Flesh pink or salmon coral. Eye Color: Deep vivid blue.

TORTIE POINT: Body creamy white or pale fawn. Points seal with unbrindled patches of red and cream. Blaze of red or cream on face is desirable. Nose Leather: Seal brown with flesh and/or coral pink mottling to conform with colors of points. Paw Pads: Seal brown with flesh and/or coral pink mottling to conform with colors of points. Eye Color: Deep vivid blue.

BLUE-CREAM POINT: Body bluish white or creamy white, shading gradually to white on the stomach and chest. Points: Blue with patches of cream. Nose Leather: Slate blue, pink, or a combination of slate blue and pink. Paw Pads: Slate blue, pink, or a combination of slate blue and pink. Eye Color: Deep vivid blue.

CHOCOLATE SOLID COLOR: Rich, warm chocolate brown, sound from roots to tip of fur. Nose Leather: Brown. Paw Pads: Brown. Eye Color: Brilliant Copper.

LILAC SOLID COLOR: Rich, warm lavendar with a pinkish tone, sound and even throughout. Nose Leather: Pink. Paw Pads: Pink. Eye Color: Brilliant Copper.

MANX

GENERAL: The overall impression of the Manx cat is that of roundness: round head with firm, round muzzle and prominent cheeks, broad chest, substantial short front legs, short back which arches from shoulders to a round rump, great depth of flank, and rounded, muscular thighs. The heavy, glossy double coat accentuates the round appearance. With regard to condition, the Manx presented in the show ring should evidence a healthy physical appearance, feeling firm and muscular, neither too fat nor too lean. The Manx should be alert, clear of eye, with a glistening, clean coat.

HEAD AND EARS: Round head with prominent cheeks and a jowly appearance. Head is slightly longer than it is broad. Moderately rounded forehead, pronounced cheekbones and jowliness (jowliness more evident in adult males) enhance the round appearance. Definite whisker break, with large, round whisker pads. In profile there is a gentle nose dip. Well-developed muzzle, slightly longer than broad, with a strong chin. Short, thick neck. Ears wide at the base, tapering gradually to a rounded tip, with sparse interior furnishings. Medium in size in proportion to the head, widely spaced and set slightly outward.

EYES: Large, round and full, set at a slight angle toward the nose (outer corners slightly higher than inner corners). Ideal eye color conforms to requirements of coat color.

BODY: Solidly muscled, compact and well-balanced, medium in size with sturdy bone structure. The Manx is stout in appearance, with broad chest and well-sprung ribs; surprisingly heavy when lifted. The constant repetition of curves and circles gives the Manx the appearance of great substance and durability, a cat that is powerful without the slightest hint of coarseness. Males may be somewhat larger than females.

Flank (fleshy area of the side between the ribs and hip) has greater depth than in any other breed, causing considerable depth to the body when viewed from the side.

The short back forms a smooth, continuous arch from shoulders to rump, curving at the rump to form the desirable round look. Shortness of back is unique to the Manx, but is in proportion to the entire cat and may be somewhat longer in the male.

TAILLESSNESS: Absolute in the perfect specimen, with a decided hollow at the end of the backbone where, in the tailed cat, a tail would begin. A rise of the bone at the end of the spine is allowed and should not be penalized unless it is such that it stops the judge's hand, thereby spoiling the tailless appearance of the cat. The rump is extremely broad and round.

LEGS AND FEET: Heavily boned, forelegs short and set well apart to emphasize the broad, deep chest. Hindlegs much longer than forelegs, with heavy, muscular thighs and substantial lower legs. Longer hindlegs cause the rump to be considerably higher than the shoulders. Hindlegs are straight when viewed from behind. Paws are neat and round, with five toes in front and four behind.

COAT: Double coat is short and dense, with a well-padded quality due to the longer, open outer coat and the close, cottony undercoat. Texture of outer guard hairs is somewhat hard; appearance is glossy. Coat may be thicker during cooler months of the year.

TRANSFER TO AOV: Definite, visible tail joint; long, silky coat.

DISQUALIFY: Evidence of poor physical condition; incorrect number of toes; evidence of hybridization; weak hind quarters causing inability to stand or walk properly.

MANX COLORS

WHITE: Pure glistening white. Nose Leather: Pink. Paw Pads: Pink. Eye Color: Deep blue or brilliant copper. Odd-eyed whites shall have one blue and one copper eye with equal color depth.

BLACK: Dense coal black, sound from roots to tip of fur. Free from any tinge of rust on tips. Nose Leather: Black. Paw Pads: Black or Brown. Eye Color: Brilliant Copper.

BLUE: Blue, lighter shade preferred, one level tone. Sound to the roots. A sound darker shade is more acceptable than an unsound lighter shade. Nose Leather: Blue. Paw Pads: Blue. Eye Color: Brilliant Copper

RED: Deep rich, clear, brilliant red; without shading, markings or ticking. Lips and chin the same color as coat. Nose Leather: Brick Red. Paw Pads: Brick Red. Eye Color: Brilliant Copper.

CREAM: One level shade of buff cream, without markings. Sound to the roots. Lighter shades preferred. Nose Leather: Pink. Paw Pads: Pink. Eye Color: Brilliant Copper

CHINCHILLA: Undercoat pure white. Coat on back, flanks, and head sufficiently tipped with black to give the characteristic sparkling silver appearance. Legs may be slightly shaded with tipping. Chin, stomach and chest, pure white. Rims of eyes, lips and nose outlined with black. Nose Leather: Brick Red. Paw Pads: Black. Eye Color: Green or Blue-Green.

SHADED SILVER: Undercoat white with a mantle of black tipping shading down from sides, and face, from dark on the ridge to white on the chin, chest, stomach. Legs to be of the same tone as the face. The general effect to be much darker than a chinchilla. Rims of eyes, lips and nose outlined with black. Nose Leather: Brick Red. Paw Pads: Black. Eye Color: Green or Blue-Green.

BLACK SMOKE: White undercoat, deeply tipped with black. Cat in repose appears black. In motion the white undercoat is clearly apparent. Points and mask black with narrow band of white at base of hairs next to skin which may be seen only when the fur is parted. Nose Leather: Black. Paw Pads: Black. Eye Color: Brilliant Copper.

BLUE SMOKE: White undercoat, deeply tipped with blue. Cat in repose appears blue. In motion the white undercoat is clearly apparent. Points and mask blue with narrow band of white at base of hairs next to skin which may be seen only when the fur is parted. Nose Leather: Blue. Paw Pads: Blue. Eye Color: Brilliant Copper.

CLASSIC TABBY PATTERN: Markings dense, clearly defined and broad. Legs evenly barred with bracelets coming up to meet the body markings. Several unbroken necklaces on neck and upper chest, the more the better. Frown marks on forehead form intricate letter "M." Unbroken line runs back from outer corner of eye. Swirls on cheeks. Vertical lines over back of head extend to shoulder markings which are in the shape of a butterfly with both upper and lower wings distinctly outlined and marked with dots inside outline. Back markings consist of a vertical line from butterfly down the entire spine with a vertical stripe paralleling it on each side, the three stripes well separated by stripes of the ground color. Large solid blotch on each side to be encircled by one or more unbroken rings. Side markings should be the same on both sides. Double vertical row of buttons on chest and stomach.

MACKEREL TABBY PATTERN: Markings dense, clearly defined, and all narrow pencillings. Legs evenly barred with narrow bracelets coming up to meet the body markings. Necklaces on neck and chest distinct, like so many chains. Head barred with an "M" on the forehead. Unbroken lines running back from the eyes. Lines running down the head to meet the shoulders. Spine lines run together to form a narrow saddle. Narrow pencillings run around body.

PATCHED TABBY PATTERN: A Patched Tabby (Torbie) is an established silver, brown, or blue tabby with patches of red and/or cream.

BROWN PATCHED TABBY: Ground color brilliant coppery brown with classic or mackerel tabby markings of dense black with patches of red and/or cream clearly defined on both body and extremities; a blaze of red and/or cream on the face is desirable. Lips and chin the same shade as the rings around the eyes. Eye Color: Brilliant Copper.

BLUE PATCHED TABBY: Ground color, including lips and chin, pale bluish ivory with classic or mackerel tabby markings of very deep blue affording a good contrast with ground color. Patches of cream clearly defined on both body and extremities; a blaze of cream on the face is desirable. Warm fawn overtones or patina over the whole. Eye Color: Brilliant Copper.

SILVER PATCHED TABBY: Ground color, including lips and chin, pale silver with classic or mackerel tabby markings of dense black with patches of red and/or cream clearly defined on both body and extremities. A blaze of red and/or cream on the face is desirable. Eye Color: Brilliant Copper or Hazel.

SILVER TABBY: Ground color, including lips and chin, pale, clear silver. Markings dense black. Nose Leather: Brick Red. Paw Pads: Black. Eye Color: Green or Hazel.

RED TABBY: Ground color red. Markings deep, rich red. Lips and chin red. Nose Leather: Brick Red. Paw Pads: Brick Red. Eye Color: Brilliant Copper.

BROWN TABBY: Ground color brilliant coppery brown. Markings dense black. Lips and chin the same shade as the rings around the eyes. Back of leg black from paw to heel. Nose Leather: Brick Red. Paw Pads: Black or Brown. Eye Color: Brilliant Copper.

BLUE TABBY: Ground color, including lips and chin, pale bluish ivory. Markings a very deep blue affording a good contrast with ground color. Warm fawn overtones or patina over the whole. Nose Leather: Old Rose. Paw Pads: Rose. Eye Color: Brilliant Copper.

CREAM TABBY: Ground color, including lips and chin, very pale cream. Markings buff or cream sufficiently darker than the ground color to afford good contrast, but remaining within the dilute color range. Nose Leather: Pink. Paw Pads: Pink. Eye Color: Brilliant Copper.

TORTOISESHELL: Black with unbrindled patches of red and cream. Patches clearly defined and well broken on both body and extremities. Blaze of red or cream on face is desirable. Eye Color: Brilliant Copper.

CALICO: White with unbrindled patches of black and red. White predominant on underparts. Eye Color: Brilliant Copper. DILUTE CALICO: White with unbrindled patches of blue and cream. White predominant on underparts. Eye Color: Brilliant copper.

BLUE-CREAM: Blue with patches of solid cream. Patches clearly defined and well broken on both body and extremities. Eye Color: Brilliant Copper.

BI-COLOR: White with unbrindled patches of black, or white with unbrindled patches of blue, or white with unbrindled patches of red, or white with unbrindled patches of cream. Cats with no more white than a locket and/or button do not qualify for this color class. Such cats shall be judged in the color class of their basic color with no penalty for such locket and/or button. Eye Color: Brilliant Copper.

OMC (Other Manx Colors): Any other color or pattern with the exception of those showing hybridization resulting in the colors chocolate, lavender, the himalayan pattern, or these combinations with white, etc. Eye Color: Appropriate to the predominant color of the cat.

PERSIAN

POINT SCORE

Head(including size and shape of eyes, ear shape and set) . . 30
Type(including shape, size, bone and length of tail 20
Coat 10
Balance 5
Refinement 5
Color 20
Eye Color 10

In all tabby varieties, the 20 points for color are to be divided 10 for markings and 10 for color.

HEAD: Round and massive, with great breadth of skull. Round face with round underlying bone structure. Well set on a short, thick neck.

EARS: Small, round tipped, tilted forward, and not unduly open at the base. Set far apart, and low on the head, fitting into (without distorting) the rounded contour of the head.

EYES: Large, round and full. Set far apart and brilliant, giving a sweet expression to the face.

NOSE: Short, snub, and broad. With "Break."

CHEEKS: Full.

JAWS: Broad and powerful.

CHIN: Full and well-developed.

BODY: Of cobby type, low on the legs, deep in the chest, equally massive across shoulders and rump, with a short, well-rounded middle piece. Large or medium in size. Quality the determining consideration, rather than size.

BACK: Level.

LEGS: Short, thick and strong. Forelegs straight.

PAWS: Large, round and firm. Toes carried close, five in front and four behind.

TAIL: Short, but in proportion to body length. Carried without a curve and at an angle lower than the back.

COAT: Long and thick, standing off from the body. Of fine texture, glossy and full of life. Long all over the body, including the shoulders. The ruff immense and continuing in a deep frill between the front legs. Ear and toe tufts long. Brush very full.

DISQUALIFY: Locket or button. Kinked or abnormal tail. Incorrect number of toes.

PERSIAN COLORS

WHITE: Pure glistening white. Nose Leather: Pink. Paw Pads: Pink. Eye Color: Deep blue or brilliant copper. Odd-eyed whites shall have one blue and one copper eye with equal color depth.

BLACK: Dense coal black, sound from roots to tip of fur.

Free from any tinge of rust on tips, or smoke undercoat. Nose Leather: Black. Paw Pads: Black or Brown. Eye Color: Brilliant Copper.

BLUE: Blue, lighter shade preferred, one level tone from nose to tip of tail. Sound to the roots. A sound darker shade is more acceptable than an unsound lighter shade. Nose Leather: Blue. Paw Pads: Blue. Eye Color: Brilliant Copper.

RED: Deep, rich, clear, brilliant red; without shading, markings or ticking. Lips and chin the same color as coat. Nose Leather: Brick Red. Paw Pads: Brick Red. Eye Color: Brilliant Copper.

CREAM: One level shade of buff cream, without markings. Sound to the roots. Lighter shades preferred. Nose Leather: Pink. Paw Pads: Pink. Eye Color: Brilliant Copper.

CHINCHILLA: Undercoat pure white. Coat on back, flanks, head, and tail sufficiently tipped with black to give the characteristic sparkling silver appearance. Legs may be slightly shaded with tipping. Chin and ear tufts, stomach and chest, pure white. Rims of eyes, lips and nose outlined with black. Nose Leather: Brick Red. Paw Pads: Black. Eye Color: Green or Blue-Green.

SHADED SILVER: Undercoat white with a mantle of black tipping shading down from sides, face, and tail from dark on the ridge to white on the chin, chest, stomach, and under the tail. Legs to be the same tone as the face. The general effect to be much darker than a chinchilla. Rims of eyes, lips and nose outlined with black. Nose Leather: Brick Red. Paw Pads: Black. Eye Color: Green or Blue-Green.

CHINCHILLA GOLDEN: Undercoat rich warm cream. Coat on back, flanks, head and tail sufficiently tipped with seal brown to give golden appearance. Legs may be slightly shaded with tipping. Chin and ear tufts, stomach and chest, cream. Rims of eyes, lips and nose outlined with seal brown. Nose Leather: Deep Rose. Paw Pads: Seal Brown. Eye Color: Green or Blue-Green.

SHADED GOLDEN: Undercoat rich warm cream with a mantle of seal brown tipping shading down from sides, face, and tail from dark on the ridge to cream on the chin, chest, stomach, and under the tail. Legs to be the same tone as the face. The general effect to be much darker than a chinchilla. Rims of eyes, lips and nose outlined with seal brown. Nose Leather: Deep Rose. Paw Pads: Seal Brown. Eye Color: Green or Blue-Green.

SHELL CAMEO (Red Chinchilla): Undercoat white, the coat on the back, flanks, head, and tail to be sufficiently tipped with red to give the characteristic sparkling appearance. Face and legs may be very slightly shaded with tipping. Chin, ear tufts, stomach, and chest white. Nose Leather: Rose. Rims of Eyes: Rose. Paw Pads: Rose. Eye Color: Brilliant Copper.

SHADED CAMEO (Red Shaded): Undercoat white with a mantle of red tipping shading down the sides, face, and tail from dark on the ridge to white on the chin, chest, stomach, and under the tail. Legs to be the same tone as face. The general effect to be much redder than the Shell Cameo. Nose Leather: Rose. Rims of Eyes: Rose. Paw Pads: Rose. Eye Color: Brilliant Copper.

SHELL TORTOISESHELL: Undercoat white. Coat on the back, flanks, head, and tail to be delicately tipped in black with well defined patches of red and cream tipped hairs as in the pattern of the Tortoiseshell. Face and legs may be slightly shaded with tipping. Chin, ear tufts, stomach, and chest white to very slightly tipped. Eye Color: Brilliant Copper. Blaze of red or cream tipping on face is desirable.

SHADED TORTOISESHELL: Undercoat white. Mantle of black tipping and clearly defined patches of red and cream tipped hairs as in the pattern of the Tortoiseshell. Shading down the sides, face, and tail from dark on the ridge to slightly tipped or white on the chin, chest, stomach, legs, and under the tail. The general effect is to be much darker than the Shell Tortoiseshell. Eye Color: Brilliant Copper. Blaze of red or cream tipping on the face is desirable.

BLACK SMOKE: White undercoat, deeply tipped with black. Cat in repose appears black. In motion the white undercoat is clearly apparent. Points and mask black with narrow band of white at base of hairs next to skin which may be seen only when the fur is parted. Light silver frill and ear tufts. Nose Leather: Black. Paw Pads: Black. Eye Color: Brilliant Copper.

BLUE SMOKE: White undercoat, deeply tipped with blue. Cat in repose appears blue. In motion the white undercoat is clearly apparent. Points and mask blue with narrow band of white at base of hairs next to skin which may be seen only when fur is parted. White frill and ear tufts. Nose Leather: Blue. Paw Pads: Blue. Eye Color: Brilliant Copper.

CAMEO SMOKE (Red Smoke): White undercoat, deeply tipped with red. Cat in repose appears red. In motion the white undercoat is clearly apparent. Points and mask red with narrow band of white at base of hairs next to skin which may be seen only when fur is parted. White frill and ear tufts. Nose Leather: Rose. Rims of Eyes: Rose. Paw Pads: Rose. Eye Color: Brilliant Copper.

SMOKE TORTOISESHELL: White undercoat deeply tipped with black with clearly defined, unbridled patches of red and cream tipped hairs as in the pattern of the Tortoiseshell. Cat in repose appears Tortoiseshell. In motion, the white undercoat is clearly apparent. Face and ears Tortoiseshell pattern with narrow band of white at the base of the hairs next to the skin that may be seen only when hair is parted. White ruff and ear tufts. Eye Color: Brilliant Copper. Blaze of red or cream tipping on face is desirable.

CLASSIC TABBY PATTERN: Markings dense, clearly defined and broad. Legs evenly barred with bracelets coming up to meet the body markings. Tail evenly ringed. Several unbroken necklaces on neck and upper chest, the more the better. Frown marks on forehead form intricate letter "M." Unbroken line runs back from outer corner of eye. Swirls on cheeks. Vertical lines over back of head extend to shoulder markings which are in the shape of a butterfly with both upper and lower wings distinctly outlined and marked with dots inside outline. Back markings consist of a vertical line down the spine from butterfly to tail with a vertical stripe paralleling it on each side, the three stripes well separated by stripes of the ground color. Large solid blotch on each side to be encircled by one or more unbroken rings. Side markings should be the same on both sides. Double vertical row of buttons on chest and stomach.

MACKEREL TABBY PATTERN: Markings dense, clearly defined, and all narrow pencillings. Legs evenly barred with narrow bracelets coming up to meet the body markings. Tail barred. Necklaces on neck and chest distinct, like so many chains. Head barred with an "M" on the forehead. Unbroken lines running back from the eyes. Lines running down the head to meet the shoulders. Spine lines run together to form a narrow saddle. Narrow pencillings run around body.

PATCHED TABBY PATTERN: A Patched Tabby (Torbie) is an established silver, brown, or blue tabby with patches of red and/or cream.

BROWN PATCHED TABBY: Ground color brilliant coppery brown with classic or mackerel tabby markings of dense black with patches of red and/or cream clearly defined on both body and extremities; a blaze of red and/or cream on the face is desirable. Lips and chin the same shade as the rings around the eyes. Eye Color: Brilliant Copper.

BLUE PATCHED TABBY: Ground color, including lips and chin, pale bluish ivory with classic or mackerel tabby markings of very deep blue affording a good contrast with ground color. Patches of cream clearly defined on both body and extremities; a blaze of cream on the face is desirable. Warm fawn overtones or patina over the whole. Eye Color: Brilliant Copper.

SILVER PATCHED TABBY: Ground color, including lips and chin, pale silver with classic or mackerel tabby markings of dense black with patches of red and/or cream clearly defined on both body and extremities. A blaze of red and/or cream on the face is desirable. Eye Color: Brilliant Copper or Hazel.

SILVER TABBY: Ground color, including lips and chin, pale, clear silver. Markings dense black. Nose Leather: Brick Red. Paw Pads: Black. Eye Color: Green or Hazel.

RED TABBY: Ground color red. Markings deep, rich red. Lips and chin red. Nose Leather: Brick Red. Paw Pads: Pink. Eye Color: Brilliant Copper.

BROWN TABBY: Ground Color brilliant coppery brown. Markings dense black. Lips and chin the same shade as the rings around the eyes. Back of leg black from paw to heel. Nose Leather: Brick Red. Paw Pads: Black or Brown. Eye Color: Brilliant Copper.

BLUE TABBY: Ground color, including lips and chin, pale bluish ivory. Markings a very deep blue affording a good contrast with ground color. Warm fawn overtones or patina over the whole. Nose Leather: Old Rose. Paw Pads: Rose. Eye Color: Brilliant Copper.

CREAM TABBY: Ground color, including lips and chin, very pale cream. Markings of buff or cream sufficiently darker than the ground color to afford good contrast, but remaining within the dilute color range. Nose Leather: Pink. Paw Pads: Pink. Eye Color: Brilliant Copper.

CAMEO TABBY: Ground color off-white. Markings red. Nose Leather: Rose. Paw Pads: Rose. Eye Color: Brilliant Copper.

TORTOISESHELL: Black with unbridled patches of red and cream. Patches clearly defined and well broken on both body and extremities. Blaze of red or cream on face is desirable. Eye Color: Brilliant Copper.

CALICO: White with unbridled patches of black and red. White predominant on underparts. Eye Color: Brilliant

Copper. DILUTE CALICO: White with unbrindled patches of blue and cream white predominant on underparts. Eye Color: Brilliant Copper.

BLUE-CREAM: Blue with patches of solid cream. Patches clearly defined and well broken on both body and extremities. Eye Color: Brilliant Copper.

BI-COLOR: Black and white, blue and white, red and white, or cream and white. White feet, legs, undersides, chest and muzzle. Inverted "V" blaze on face desirable. White under tail and white collar allowable. Eye Color: Brilliant Copper.

PERSIAN VAN BI-COLOR: Black and white, red and white, blue and white, cream and white. White cat with color confined to the extremities; head, tail, and legs. One or two small colored patches on body allowable.

PEKE-FACE RED AND PEKE-FACE RED TABBY: The Peke-Face cat should conform in color, markings and general type to the standards set forth for the red and red tabby Persian cat. The head should resemble as much as possible that of the Pekinese dog from which it gets its name. Nose should be very short and depressed, or indented between the eyes. There should be a decidedly wrinkled muzzle. Eyes round, large, and full, set wide apart, prominent and brilliant.

PERSIAN VAN CALICO: White cat with unbrindled patches of black and red confined to the extremities; head, tail, and legs. One or two small colored patches on body allowable.

PERSIAN VAN BLUE—CREAM AND WHITE: White cat with unbrindled patches of blue and cream confined to the extremities; head, tail, and legs. One or two· small colored patches on body allowable.

Note: Cats possessing more than a couple of small body spots should be shown in the regular Bi-Color class.

SIAMESE

GENERAL: The ideal Siamese is a medium-sized, svelte, dainty cat with long, tapering lines, very lithe but muscular.

HEAD: Long tapering wedge. Medium size in good proportion to body. The total wedge starts at the nose and flares out in straight lines to the tips of the ears forming a triangle, with no break at the whiskers. No less than the width of an eye between the eyes. When the whiskers are smoothed back, the underlying bone structure is apparent. Allowance must be made for jowls in the stud cat.

SKULL: Flat. In profile, a long straight line is seen from the top of the head to the tip of the nose. No bulge over eyes. No dip in nose.

EARS: Strikingly large, pointed, wide at base, continuing the lines of the wedge.

EYES: Almond shaped. Medium size. Neither protruding nor recessed. Slanted towards the nose in harmony with lines of wedge and ears. Uncrossed.

NOSE: Long and straight. A continuation of the forehead with no break.

MUZZLE: Fine, wedge-shaped.

CHIN AND JAW: Medium size. Tip of chin lines up with tip of nose in the same vertical plane. Neither receding nor excessively massive.

BODY: Medium size. Dainty, long, and svelte. A distinctive combination of fine bones and firm muscles Shoulders and hips continue same sleek lines of tubular body. Hips never wider than shoulders. Abdomen tight.

NECK: Long and slender.

LEGS: Long and slim. Hind legs higher than front. In good proportion to body.

PAWS: Dainty, small, and oval. Toes, five in front and four behind.

TAIL: Long, thin, tapering to a fine point.

COAT: Short, fine textured, glossy. Lying close to body.

CONDITION: Excellent physical condition. Eyes clear. Muscular, strong and lithe. Neither flabby nor boney. Not fat.

COLOR: Body: Even, with subtle shading when allowed. Allowance should be made for darker color in older cats as Siamese generally darken with age, but there must be definite contrast between body color and points. Points: Mask, ears, legs, feet, tail dense and clearly defined. All of the same shade. Mask covers entire face including whisker pads and is connected to ears by tracings. Mask should not extend over the top of the head. No ticking or white hairs in points.

PENALIZE: Improper (i.e., off-color or spotted) nose leather or paw pads. Soft or mushy body.

DISQUALIFY: Any evidence of illness or poor health. Weak hind legs. Mouth breathing due to nasal obstruction or to poor occlusion. Emaciation. Visible kink. Eyes other than blue. White toes and/or feet. Incorrect number of toes. Malocclusion resulting in either undershot or overshot chin.

SIAMESE COLORS

SEAL POINT: Body even pale fawn to cream, warm in tone, shading gradually into lighter color on the stomach and chest. Points deep seal brown. Nose Leather: Same color as points. Paw Pads: Same color as points. Eye Color: Deep vivid blue.

CHOCOLATE POINT: Body ivory with no shading. Points milk-chocolate color, warm in tone. Nose Leather: Cinnamon-Pink. Paw Pads: Cinnamon-Pink. Eye Color: Deep vivid blue.

BLUE POINT: Body bluish white, cold in tone, shading gradually to white on stomach and chest. Points deep blue. Nose Leather: Slate colored. Paw Pads: Slate colored. Eye Color: Deep vivid blue.

LILAC POINT: Body glacial white with no shading. Points frosty grey with pinkish tone. Nose Leather: Lavender-Pink. Paw Pads: Lavender-Pink. Eye Color: Deep vivid blue.

HAVANA BROWN

GENERAL: The overall impression of the ideal Havana Brown is a cat of medium size with a rich, solid color and good muscle tone. Due to its distinctive muzzle shape, color and large forward-tilted ears, it is comparable to no other breed.

HEAD: The head is slightly longer than it is wide, with a distinct stop at the eyes. The break at the whisker pad is about the same width overall. A strong chin forms a straight line with the nose. Allowance will be made for stud jowls in the male.

COAT: The coat is medium in length, smooth, and lustrous.

BODY AND NECK: Body and neck are medium in length, firm and muscular. The general conformation is mid-range between the short-coupled, thick-set and svelte breeds.

EYES: Oval Shaped.

EARS: Ears are large, wide set, round tipped, slightly tilted forward, not flaring, giving an alert appearance. They have little hair inside or out.

LEGS AND FEET: Medium in length, ending in oval paw pads.

TAIL: Medium to medium long, tapering.

COLOR: Rich, warm, mahogany toned brown. Solid to the roots; free from tabby markings or barring in the adult. Nose Leather: brown with a rosy cast. Paw Pads: having a rosy tone. Eyes: ranging from chartreuse to green, with the greener shades preferred. Whiskers: brown, complementing the coat.

DISQUALIFY: Kinked tail, locket or button, incorrect eye color, whisker, nose leather or paw pad color.

REX

HEAD (25)

Size and Shape	5
Muzzle and Nose	5
Eyes	5
Ears	5
Profile	5

BODY (30)

Size	3
Torso	10
Legs and Paws	5
Tail	5
Bone	5
Neck	2

COAT (40)

Texture	10
Length	5
Wave, Extent of Wave	20
Close Lying	5

COLOR (5)

GENERAL: The Rex is distinguised from all other breeds by its extremely soft, wavy coat and racy type. It is surprisingly heavy and warm to the touch. All contours of the Rex are gently curved. By nature, the Rex is intelligent, alert, and generaly likes to be handled.

PROFILE: A curve comprised of two convex arcs. The forehead is rounded, the nose break smooth and mild, and the Roman nose has a high prominent bridge.

HEAD: Comparatively small and narrow; length about one-third greater than the width. A definite whisker break.

MUZZLE: Narrowing slightly to a rounded end.

EARS: Large and full from the base, erect and alert; set high on the head.

EYES: Medium to large in size, oval in shape and slanting slightly upward. A full eye's width apart. Color should be clear, intense and appropriate to coat color.

NOSE: Roman. Length is one-third length of head. In profile a straight line from end of nose to chin with considerable depth and squarish effect.

CHEEKS: Lean and muscular.

CHIN: Strong, well-developed.

BODY: Small to medium, males proportionately larger. Torso long and slender, not tubular; hips, muscular and somewhat heavy in proportion to the rest of the body. Back is naturally arched with lower line of the body approaching the upward curve. The arch is evident when the cat is standing naturally.

SHOULDERS: Well knit.

RUMP: Rounded, well muscled.

LEGS: Very long and slender. Hips well muscled, somewhat heavy in proportion to the rest of the body. The Rex stands high on its legs.

PAWS: Dainty, slightly oval. Toes, five in front and four behind.

TAIL: Long and slender, tapering toward the end and extremely flexible.

NECK: Long and slender.

BONE: Fine and delicate.

COAT: Short, extremely soft, silky, and completely free of guard hairs. Relatively dense. A tight, uniform marcel wave, lying close to the body and extending from the top of the head across the back, sides, and hips continuing to the tip of the tail. The fur on the underside of the chin and on chest and abdomen is short and noticeably wavy.

CONDITION: Firm and muscular.

DISQUALIFY: Kinked or abnormal tail. Incorrect number of toes. Any coarse or guard hairs. Evidence of hybridization resulting in the colors chocolate, lavender, the Himalayan pattern or these combinations with white.

REX COLORS

WHITE: Pure glistening white. Nose Leather: Pink. Paw Pads: Pink. Eye Color: Deep blue or brilliant gold. Odd-eyed whites shall have one blue and one gold eye with equal color depth.

BLACK: Dense coal black, sound from roots to tip of fur. Free from any tinge of rust on tips. Nose Leather: Black. Paw Pads: Black or Brown. Eye Color: Gold

BLUE: Blue, lighter shade preferred, one level tone from nose to tip of tail. Sound to the roots. A sound darker shade is more acceptable than an unsound lighter shade. Nose Leather: Blue. Paw Pads: Blue. Eye Color: Gold

RED: Deep, rich, clear, brilliant red; without shading, markings or ticking. Lips and chin the same color as the coat. Nose Leather: Brick Red. Paw Pads: Brick Red. Eye Color: Gold

CREAM: One level shade of buff cream, without markings. Sound to the roots. Lighter shades preferred. Nose Leather: Pink. Paw Pads: Pink. Eye Color: Gold

CHINCHILLA: Undercoat pure white. Coat on back, flanks, head and tail sufficiently tipped with black to give the characteristic sparkling silver appearance. Legs may be slightly shaded with tipping. Chin, stomach and chest, pure white. Rims of eyes, lips and nose outlined with black. Nose Leather: Brick Red. Paw Pads: Black. Eye Color: Green or Blue-Green.

SHADED SILVER: Undercoat white with a mantle of black tipping shading down from sides, face, and tail from dark on the ridge to white on the chin, chest, stomach, and under the tail. Legs to be the same tone as the face. The general effect to be much darker than a chinchilla. Rims of eyes, lips and nose outlined with black. Nose Leather: Brick Red. Paw Pads: Black. Eye Color: Green or Blue-Green.

BLACK SMOKE: White undercoat, deeply tipped with black. Cat in repose appears black. In motion the white undercoat is clearly apparent. Points and mask black with narrow band of white at base of hairs next to skin which may be seen only when the fur is parted. Nose Leather: Black. Paw Pads: Black. Eye Color: Gold

BLUE SMOKE: White undercoat, deeply tipped with blue. Cat in repose appears blue. In motion the white undercoat is clearly apparent. Points and mask blue with narrow band of white at base of hairs next to skin which may be seen only when fur is parted. Nose Leather: Blue. Paw Pads: Blue. Eye Color: Gold

CLASSIC TABBY PATTERN: Markings dense, clearly defined and broad. Legs evenly barred with bracelets coming up to meet the body markings. Tail evenly ringed. Several unbroken necklaces on neck and upper chest, the more the better. Frown marks on forehead form intricate letter "M." Unbroken line runs back from outer corner of eye. Swirls on cheeks. Vertical lines over back of head extend to shoulder markings which are in the shape of a butterfly with both upper and lower wings distinctly outlined and marked with dots inside outline. Back markings consist of a vertical line down the spine from butterfly to tail with a vertical stripe paralleling it on each side, the three stripes well separated by stripes of the ground color. Large solid blotch on each side to be encircled by one or more unbroken rings. Side markings should be the same on both sides. Double vertical row of buttons on chest and stomach.

MACKEREL TABBY PATTERN: Markings dense, clearly defined, and all narrow pencillings. Legs evenly barred with narrow bracelets coming up to meet the body markings. Tail barred. Necklaces on neck and chest distinct, like so many chains. Head barred with an "M" on the forehead. Unbroken lines running back from the eyes. Lines running down the head to meet the shoulders. Spine lines run together to form a narrow saddle. Narrow pencillings run around body.

PATCHED TABBY PATTERN: A Patched Tabby (Torbie) is an established silver, brown, or blue tabby with patches of red and/or cream.

BROWN PATCHED TABBY: Ground color brilliant coppery brown with classic or mackerel tabby markings of dense black with patches of red and/or cream clearly defined on both body and extremities; a blaze of red and/or cream on the face is desirable. Lips and chin the same shade as the rings around the eyes. Eye Color: Brilliant Gold.

SILVER TABBY: Ground color, including lips and chin, pale, clear silver. Markings dense black. Nose Leather: Brick Red. Paw Pads: Black. Eye Color: Green or Hazel.

RED TABBY: Ground color red. Markings deep, rich red. Lips and chin red. Nose Leather: Brick Red. Paw Pads: Brick Red. Eye Color: Gold

BROWN TABBY: Ground color brilliant coppery brown. Markings dense black. Lips and chin the same shade as the rings around the eyes. Back of leg black from paw to heel. Nose Leather: Brick Red. Paw Pads: Black or Brown. Eye Color: Gold

BLUE TABBY: Ground color, including lips and chin, pale, bluish ivory. Markings a very deep blue affording a good contrast with ground color. Warm fawn overtones or patina over the whole. Nose Leather: Old Rose. Paw Pads: Rose. Eye Color: Gold

CREAM TABBY: Ground color, including lips and chin, very pale cream. Markings buff or cream sufficiently darker than the ground color to afford good contrast, but remaining within the dilute color range. Nose Leather: Pink. Paw Pads: Pink. Eye Color: Gold

TORTOISESHELL: Black with unbrindled patches of red and cream. Patches clearly defined and well broken on both body and extremities. Blaze of red or cream on face is desirable. Eye Color: Gold

CALICO: White with unbrindled patches of black and red. White predominant on underparts. Eye Color: Gold. DILUTE CALICO: White with unbrindled patches of blue and cream, white predominant on underparts. Eye Color: Gold.

BLUE-CREAM: Blue with patches of solid cream. Patches clearly defined and well broken on both body and extremities. Eye Color: Gold

BI-COLOR: White with unbrindled patches of black, or white with unbrindled patches of blue, or white with unbrindled patches of red, or white with unbrindled patches of cream. Cats with no more white than a locket and/or button do not qualify for this color class. Such cats shall be judged in the color class of their basic color with no penalty for such locket and/or button. Eye Color: Gold

ORC (Other Rex Colors): Any other color or pattern with the exception of those showing evidence of hybridization resulting in the colors chocolate, lavender, the himalayan pattern, or these combinations with white, etc. Eye Color: Appropriate to the predominant color of the cat.

BLUE PATCHED TABBY: Ground color, including lips and chin, pale bluish ivory with classic or mackerel tabby markings of very deep blue affording a good contrast with ground color. Patches of cream clearly defined on both body and extremities; a blaze of cream on the face is desirable. Warm fawn overtones or patina over the whole. Eye Color: Brilliant Gold.

SILVER PATCHED TABBY: Ground color, including lips and chin, pale silver with classic or mackerel tabby markings of dense black with patches of red and/or cream clearly defined on both body and extremities. A blaze of red and/or cream on the face is desirable. Eye Color: Brilliant Gold or Hazel.

RUSSIAN BLUE

POINT SCORE

Head and Neck 20
Body Type 20
Eye Shape 5
Ears 5
Coat 20
Color 20
Eye Color 10

GENERAL: The good show specimen has good physical condition, is firm in muscle tone, and alert.

HEAD: Top of skull flat and long. The face is broad across the eyes due to wide eye-set and thick fur.

MUZZLE: Smooth, flowing wedge without prominent whisker pads or whisker pinches.

EARS: Rather large and wide at the base. Tips more pointed than rounded. The skin of the ears is thin and translucent, with little inside furnishing. The outside of the ear is scantily covered with short, very fine hair, with leather showing through. Set far apart, as much on the side as on the top of the head.

EYES: Set wide apart. Aperture rounded in shape.

NECK: Long and slender, but appearing short due to thick fur and high placement of shoulder blades.

NOSE: Medium in length.

CHIN: Perpendicular with the end of the nose and with level under-chin. Neither receding nor excessively massive.

BODY: Fine boned, long, firm and muscular, lithe and graceful in outline and carriage.

LEGS: Long and fine-boned.

PAWS: Small, slightly rounded. Toes, five in front and four behind.

TAIL: Long, but in proportion to the body. Tapering from a moderately thick base.

COAT: Short, dense, fine and plush. Double coat stands out from body due to density. It has a distinct soft and silky feel.

COLOR: Even bright blue throughout. Lighter shades of blue preferred. Guard hairs distinctly silver-tipped giving the cat a silvery sheen or lustrous appearance. A definite contrast should be noted between ground color and tipping. Free from tabby markings. Nose Leather: Slate Grey. Paw Pads: Lavender-Pink or Mauve. Eye Color: Vivid Green.

DISQUALIFY: Kinked or abnormal tail. Locket or button. Incorrect number of toes.

The Cat's World

Cats are naturally curious and like to explore new places and things. Their curiosity is often their undoing—"curiosity killed a cat ..." The last part of this adage, "... satisfaction brought him back," is not necessarily true. Cats are, however, very quick at catching on. Once they have investigated a hot stove or a cigarette, all stoves and all cigarettes are taboo.

Because of their curiosity, cats are what we may sometimes consider "destructive." They are also destructive because of other instincts: the instinct to scratch and flex their claws; to pounce on moving objects, then shred them; to get their food by theft. They are destructive from sheer playfulness. To minimize torn furniture, a scratching post should be provided and every time the cat scratches the furniture, take the animal to the post.

Toys and an old sock or rag doll of its very own will satisfy most of your cat's chewing and gnawing and will keep it away from your better things. If you give a cat an old sock to chew, it won't (contrary to some opinions) think *all* socks are meant for chewing. "Pride of possession" will satisfy your pet.

TRAVELING AND SHIPPING

Cats are great travelers. All but a very few like to travel by car. Those who don't are generally older cats who have never done it before. When traveling in the car, be sure that your cat is leashed and that no windows are open wide enough for the animal to jump through. Also, be careful that it doesn't annoy the driver. When driving alone with your pet or pets, put it or them in a cat carrier.

The cat carrier, which is relatively inexpensive, makes it much easier at all times to transport even one cat, especially if otherwise you would have to carry it in your arms. You can instead buy a wicker basket, with a lid—the weave lets in air. Most cats do not mind this form of travel. Koki (a Siamese of mine) used to run and sit by her leash when she wanted to go out; after she had ridden in the carrier a couple of times, she would run and sit by that or, if the lid was up, jump in!

When traveling by train, a cat carrier is a necessity. It is better to have your cat with you than to check it in the baggage car, where it will be subjected to drafts and frightening noises. Some cats will go out cheerfully in boats. Booty-Too, a domestic shorthair, loved rowboats. Most cats like planes too.

Your kittens should be trained to travel in a cat carrier at an early age. Cats and kittens are usually excellent travelers. Your local pet shop will usually have a nice selection of wicker and other types of cat carriers.

It is better to use a harness than a collar for walking a cat, and for car travel the harness is ninety-nine per cent better. If the cat should slip or take a tumble, you know it won't break its neck.

When shipping cats, crate them well, mark the crate with the contents and insure it for the cat's value (or more). Ship *only* by Air Express and never around the holiday season. Either you or someone else should be waiting at the other end for the cat's arrival.

Since cats are relatively little trouble when traveling by car, and since they are acceptable in many motels, it is better to bring your cat with you, if possible, than to leave it behind with a friend or at a boarding kennel. Feeding en route is no problem—most cats will eat on the floor of the car, from their dish. Your cat's pan can be put on the floor in the back of the car, and in no time it will learn to use it when the car is in motion. It'll pick anywhere to sleep—my cats usually sleep on the rear window deck or in the crown of my husband's hat!

When going into a motel, bring in the cat and the pan first, put them in the bathroom and shut the door. Check first to make sure the window is closed. This will keep your pet from running out of the door or from getting underfoot while you bring in your luggage. After you've closed all the doors for the final time, let your pet out of the bathroom to explore for a few minutes; then feed it. It will quickly adapt to the new surroundings.

CATS AND DOGS

If you already have a dog, it is perfectly fine to bring in your new cat or kitten. First, however, make sure the cat's claws have been trimmed. Do not rush in and present Fido with his new playmate, but do not hide them from each other. Try not to give Fido any less attention, although that will be hard to do.

A kitten should adjust faster to the dog, and a young dog will adjust better to a cat than an old one. Getting a puppy and a kitten at the same time works out well, as they are both young and so busy getting acquainted with their new surroundings that they haven't time to fight! Most dogs will learn very quickly to respect a cat, and in no time they will be fast friends. As soon as you see them playing together and sleeping together, you can relax.

Cats and dogs have a fine sense of ownership and priority. To illustrate, there were once two cats, Blackie and Lex, and two dogs, Tom and Sam. Tom and Sam lived in the left hand half of a duplex house, with the cats in the other. This house had a common porch, with two separate sets of stairs. Blackie, Lex, Tom and Sam took their walks together and hunted, visited and played together. When it was time to go

Three beautiful portraits of cream long-haired kittens exhibiting their irresistible charm.

This Manx is illustrating a cat's fine sense of balance. Its movements would be graceful enough for a ballet dancer! Photo by Sally Anne Thompson. Below: Sometimes cats and dogs become better friends than their owners, because pets usually spend more time with each other.

home every night they would separate at the bottom of the porch, the dogs going up their steps and Blackie and Lex going up theirs. When they slept or sunned themselves on the porch, none of them would cross the invisible center line, even to play. They would all solemnly walk down their own stairs and *then* meet for recreation.

Cats and dogs cooperate too. One example of this was Beta, a Manx. Beta lived in an apartment, near some woods. Except for a large English bulldog, he was the only animal in the area, he thought. So, Beta and the dog became acquaintances. Then one day as Beta was out sunning himself, a large black cat appeared from the woods and began chasing him, 'round and 'round the building. Beta couldn't get away, nor did he dare stop running. Suddenly he spied his friend the bulldog sunning himself. Beta ran up behind the sleeping dog and waited for the interloper to catch up. Sure enough, around the corner of the apartment came the black cat, with fire in his eye, intent on getting Beta. But, he came to a sudden halt—he had seen the dog!

A domestic shorthair and a mutt showing mutual affection for one another! If a particular dog and cat have a friendship, it doesn't mean that another animal would be equally welcome as a friend.

Puppies and kittens tolerate each other better than adult dogs and cats. This photograph shows two young pets being introduced. Their poses indicate a mutual curiosity.

This young Havana Brown appears to be totally absorbed in whatever has caught its attention.

The two light-colored young cats in this group of three are Rex kittens. Photos this page by Fritz Prenzel.

Cream longhair kitten.

Cream longhair kitten.

CATS AND OTHER CATS

Cats and cats, and kittens and cats (other than direct off-spring), adjust differently and more vocally than dogs and cats. Oddly enough, it is generally the newcomer who raises the most ruckus. It is scared and has *so* many things on its mind that it seems to jump at its own shadow. The already settled-in cat is on familiar ground and generally not frightened, only protective of what is his. Very frequently the older cat who "belongs" will object to the new one's use of his eating and sleeping areas, pan and even your lap.

A kitten seems to adjust in a couple of days, a grown cat in a week or two. Never force the cats together; give them separate dishes (of course, each will think the other's better and exchange); cuddle them separately, and so on. As with dogs, give the first-owned more attention than usual. The new cat will be too excited to have this do it much good, and your older cat will need it. By this, I don't mean to ignore the little stranger—no doubt it is too cute to resist. Do, however, try to be fair. After the cats have eaten and slept together peaceably, all is well. They are a team now and devoted to each other. They will band together to run out other "unwanted guests."

Two of my cats, Koki and Pan, have found a new way of attacking intruders. Often the intruding cat will run under a low object and hide, where it is "safe." Koki runs in front of the skulking cat, luring it out; and Pan, the fighter, chases him away.

When we first brought home one of our studs, Phra Shri Yhu Tu (Siamese) the other cats didn't know what to make of him. They were friendly at first, until his growl and hiss (the biggest parts of him, as he was a "wee kit") made them wary. Then, he settled down and, after several days, they forgot his ill manners and accepted him socially. After a few weeks, he became their "baby"—they fought for him and washed him for all the world like little girls with a new doll.

It is amazing what games cats will play together. Like children, they compete in jumping, racing, climbing and other games of skill. They also play tag, follow-the-leader, hide and go seek and other obviously "fun" games.

If a guest comes to your house with a cat, it is best to ignore all of the cats. They'll growl and usually both sides will declare a truce and hide. Many times if you have feline visitors who use the litter pan, your cat may run in and dig out all the sand after the guest has left. Then, it won't relieve itself until the pan is refilled.

HAVING KITTENS

Most cats have no difficulty delivering kittens. It is a natural thing and should be treated as such. However, there are a few pointers to keep in mind.

If possible, before she is bred, have your female checked by a veterinarian. If she is a small cat or has had a case of rickets, she may not be able to deliver the kittens properly. Also, have her checked at least once during her pregnancy. At about the fifth week of pregnancy, give the prospective mother more food. Give her (especially) milk—as much as she'll drink—and beef and eggs (only the yolks, if given raw). Give her about one teaspoonful of butter, corn oil or olive oil every second or third day as a preventive for constipation. She should have exercise—but not strenuous leaping or jumping.

A cat carries her kittens about sixty-three days. In a young queen they may be born about the fifty-eighth or sixtieth day; in an old cat perhaps up to the sixty-fourth or sixty-fifth day. A veterinarian is generally not needed, but it is wise to have one on call, especially if it is the cat's (and your) first experience. If her time goes past sixty-five days, call the vet. If the queen is in labor for more than four hours, is bleeding excessively, is having difficulties expelling the kittens or seems really *sick*, call your vet immediately.

Above and below: two cute tabby shorthairs.

The kittens are expelled in a membranous sack, which the mother cat normally eats. The size of the litter may range from only one kitten to as many as eight, but either of these extremes is rare; the average litter consists of four or five kittens. After the kittens are born, leave them alone with the mother cat when you have ascertained: that they will not be smothered; that they are in a place small enough so the kittens cannot become misplaced; and that the mother cat has enough milk with which to feed them. The latter is assured by gently pressing her teats between forefinger and thumb. If a drop of milk shows, all is well. Most cats are well prepared by nature for this, but if there is no milk appearing within six hours, call your veterinarian.

If there are too many kittens or if any kitten is dead or deformed, remove the unwanted ones immediately. Have your veterinarian or the ASPCA put them away quickly and painlessly. Leave at least one kitten for her. Do not remove all the cat's kittens, unless it is absolutely necessary—if they are all born dead or if the mother cat is too ill to care for them (to be decided only by a veterinarian). In this event, it will be necessary for you to massage the milk out of the mother cat's nipples frequently. Your vet will tell you how often to do this and will show you how.

As the queen nurses her young, she should get the same food as she was fed when pregnant. After approximately three weeks, you may start decreasing the number of feedings and increasing the rations, so at six to eight weeks after the kittens have been born the cat is back to normal but still vitaminized feedings. From then on the mother cat

A lovely blue-cream longhair queen with her cream kittens and blue kittens.

Whiskers forward, shown in the photograph to the left, indicates curiosity. The forward, perked ears show the kitten is being attentive. In the photo below, the cat has a look on its face which is hard to distinguish between "just resting" and "I'm waiting for a mouse."

This Manx is waiting patiently to go outside to relieve itself. The posture indicates that intent.

will train and wean the kits by herself, with a little help from you. When the kittens are three weeks old, you may begin feeding them a little scraped raw beef and other such foods as described in the chapter on feeding (under the heading "The First Year").

CAT COMMUNICATION

Now for a bit about how your cat converses. A cat talks to other cats by its facial expressions, some of them too delicate for us to even notice. A cat talks to other cats with its eyes, whiskers and body. Its "meow" is primarily for conveying messages to people, who just can't seem to understand a cat otherwise.

Some of the more obvious signs cats use are:
Fluffed up tail—fright
Tail drooping—disgust or fatigue, possible ill health
Lashing tail—anger or annoyance
Tail in the air—gay, good health
Growl—anger
Purr—contentment
A light, upwardly inflected "meow"—a question. When addressed to another cat, usually means "Come play."
Ears flattened against head—intense anger
Ears tilted backward—displeasure
Ears pricked far forward—attention
Whiskers forward—curiosity
Rubbing of whiskers on you or an object—love or desire
Fur ruffled up—too cold, or ill health

No, this queen is not growling in protection of her kitten; she is just stretching after a nap. Photo by Sally Anne Thompson.

This rare photograph shows the original wild cat from which all the cats we know as pets have descended.

A trio of uniformly bred white Persian kittens.

Your cat's ears also act as miniature radar units, turning toward sounds.

After a cat returns from outdoors, and its feline companion has remained in the house, the first thing it will do is hunt up its little buddy and touch noses. This is reassurance that all is well and as it should be.

If your "family" has consisted of more than one cat and, for one reason or another, its number has been decreased, for several days the cat who remains will hunt through the house, meowing and crying, looking for its friend.

You will soon grow accustomed to the behavior of your own pet and know what it means—as it will cope with yours—and your happiness together will thrive.

IN CONCLUSION

Cats *can* get along with no care at all from humans. They may also leave an otherwise happy home because of too much coddling. Generally, cats love attention though, and the more you give your cats, the friendlier they will be.

Cats enjoy love—and lots of it. They don't care if you love them in a hut or a palace, and they don't care whether they eat from tin dishes or bone china. They don't care about your background or your job, so long as you have time for them. They'll adjust their hours to yours and alter their mealtimes to suit your convenience so long as the feedings are regular.

Properly cared for, your kitten will grow into a healthy, adult feline companion—your best buddy.